Oster Digital Air Fryer Oven Cookbook for Beginners

800-Day Crispy, Quick & Easy Recipes to Fry, Bake, Grill & Roast Most Wanted Family Meals

Fiphan Tebans

© Copyright 2021 Fiphan Tebans - All Rights Reserved.

In no way is it legal to reproduce, duplicate, or transmit any part of this document by either electronic means or in printed format. Recording of this publication is strictly prohibited, and any storage of this material is not allowed unless with written permission from the publisher. All rights reserved.

The information provided herein is stated to be truthful and consistent, in that any liability, regarding inattention or otherwise, by any usage or abuse of any policies, processes, or directions contained within is the solitary and complete responsibility of the recipient reader. Under no circumstances will any legal liability or blame be held against the publisher for any reparation, damages, or monetary loss due to the information herein, either directly or indirectly.

Respective authors own all copyrights not held by the publisher.

Legal Notice:

This book is copyright protected. This is only for personal use. You cannot amend, distribute, sell, use, quote or paraphrase any part of the content within this book without the consent of the author or copyright owner. Legal action will be pursued if this is breached.

Disclaimer Notice:

Please note the information contained within this document is for educational and entertainment purposes only. Every attempt has been made to provide accurate, up-to-date and reliable, complete information. No warranties of any kind are expressed or implied. Readers acknowledge that the author is not engaging in the rendering of legal, financial, medical or professional advice.

By reading this document, the reader agrees that under no circumstances are we responsible for any losses, direct or indirect, which are incurred as a result of the use of information contained within this document, including, but not limited to, errors, omissions, or inaccuracies.

Table of Contents

Introduction 5
Chapter 1: Breakfast & Brunch 6

- Broccoli Asparagus Frittata 6
- Banana Oat Muffins 7
- Nutritious Egg Breakfast Muffins 8
- Choco Chip Banana Bread............... 9
- Easy Cheese Egg Casserole 10
- Spinach Egg Bites.......................... 11
- Baked Breakfast Quiche.................. 12
- Easy Breakfast Bake 13
- Breakfast Sweet Potato Hash 14
- Ham Egg Muffins 15
- Lemon Blueberry Bread 16
- Flavorful Pumpkin Bread................. 17
- Breakfast Oatmeal Cake.................. 18
- Spinach Zucchini Egg Muffins........ 19
- Easy Egg Quiche............................ 20

Chapter 2: Poultry.. 21

- Bacon Broccoli Chicken 21
- Simple & Healthy Baked Chicken Breasts 22
- Pesto Chicken 23
- Baked Italian Lemon Chicken......... 24
- Baked Spinach Cheese Chicken...... 25
- Greek Chicken Breast 26
- Zucchini Chicken Meatballs 27
- Meatballs 28
- Meatballs 29
- Air Fry Chicken Drumsticks 30
- Meatballs 31
- Garlic Butter Wings 32
- Honey Chicken Wings.................... 33
- Simple Jerk Chicken Wings............ 34
- Garlic Chicken Wings 35

Chapter 3: Beef, Pork & Lamb 36

- Juicy & Tender Pork Chops 36
- Meatloaf 37
- Meatballs 38
- Meatloaf 39
- Air Fryer Herb Pork Chops 40
- Crispy Cracker Crusted Pork Chops 41
- Meatballs 42
- Jalapeno Basil Lamb Patties 43
- Simple Burger Patties 44
- Meatballs 45
- Meatballs 46
- Flavorful Sirloin Steak 47
- Crispy Crusted Pork Chops............ 48
- Meatballs 49
- Easy Pork Bites 50

Chapter 4: Fish & Seafood 51

- Marinated Salmon 51
- Paprika Cod 52
- Miso White Fish Fillets................... 53
- Delicious Baked Basa 54
- Moist & Juicy Baked Cod............... 55
- Spicy Baked Shrimp 56
- Italian Salmon 57
- Tender & Juicy Cajun Cod 58
- Parmesan Salmon & Asparagus...... 59
- Basil Tomato Salmon...................... 60
- Italian Cod 61
- Tasty Lemon Pepper Basa 62
- Perfect Crab Cakes......................... 63
- Spinach Scallops............................ 64
- Quick Tuna Patties 65

Chapter 5: Vegetables & Side Dishes................................ 66

- Cheesy Squash Casserole............... 66
- Tasty Butternut Squash 67
- Baked Paprika Sweet Potatoes 68
- Baked Potatoes & Carrots 69
- Baked Vegetables 70
- Healthy Spinach Muffins 71
- Tasty Hassel Back Potatoes 72
- Healthy Green Beans 73
- Brussels Sprouts & Sweet Potatoes. 74
- Baked Turnip & Sweet Potato 75
- Cheese Herb Zucchini 76
- Air Fry Garlic Baby Potatoes........... 77
- Air-Fried Herb Mushrooms 78
- Easy Broccoli Bread....................... 79
- Chili Lime Sweet Potatoes 80

Chapter 6: Snacks & Appetizers 81
    Delicious Cauliflower Hummus 81
    Creamy Chicken Dip 82
    Baked Almonds 83
    Bacon Cheese Jalapeno Poppers..... 84
    Cheddar Dill Mushrooms 85
    Cheesy Spinach Dip 86
    Garlic Cauliflower Florets 87
    Kale Chips 88
    Shrimp Kebabs 89
    Spicy Chicken Wings 90
    Artichoke Cashews Spinach Dip 91
    Air Fryer Radish Chips 92
    Coconut Broccoli Pop-Corn 93
    Habanero Chicken Wings 94
    Zucchini Coconut Bites 95

Chapter 7: Desserts 96
    Cinnamon Apple Crisp 96
    Peanut Butter Muffins 97
    Apple Cake 98
    Vanilla Butter Cake 99
    Vanilla Lemon Cupcakes 100
    Easy Blueberry Muffins 101
    Simple Lemon Pie 102
    Mini Brownie Muffins 103
    Coconut Butter Apple Bars 104
    Vanilla Banana Brownies 105
    Tasty Gingersnap Cookies 106
    Delicious Raspberry Cobbler 107
    Almond Butter Cookies 108
    Strawberry Muffins 109
    Almond Pecan Cookies 110

Conclusion 111

Introduction

I bet you crave simple, complete Digital Air Fryer Oven recipes! That's why I decided to create the best air fryer cookbook with 800 delicious & easy meals, that you'll ever need to cook in your Digital Air Fryer Oven! The recipes are clear and easy to follow, even for a beginner. You don't have to spend much time cooking because you can make a delicious meal for the whole family in just 30 minutes!

This cookbook consists of fun and important tips and tricks. In this cookbook, you will be offered a wide range of amazing and delicious recipes that you can cook with your prized Digital Air Fryer Oven. These recipes are detailed to the exact ratio of all ingredients, as well as the weight. Make good use of it and start making healthier fried food.

This Digital Air Fryer Oven cookbook will take care of your scarce cooking time and will show you the easiest & tastiest way towards a whole new life with your Digital Air Fryer Oven.

Chapter 1: Breakfast & Brunch

Broccoli Asparagus Frittata

Preparation Time: 10 minutes
Cooking Time: 20 minutes
Serve: 6

Ingredients:

- 6 eggs
- 1/2 cup onion, diced & sautéed
- 1 cup asparagus, chopped & sautéed
- 1 cup broccoli, chopped & sautéed
- 3 bacon slices, cooked & chopped
- 1/3 cup parmesan cheese, grated
- 1/2 cup milk
- 1/2 tsp pepper
- 1 tsp salt

Directions:

1. Fit the Oster oven with the rack in position 1.
2. In a mixing bowl, whisk eggs with milk, cheese, pepper, and salt.
3. Add onion, asparagus, broccoli, and bacon and stir well.
4. Pour egg mixture into the greased baking dish.
5. Set to bake at 350 F for 25 minutes. After 5 minutes place the baking dish in the preheated oven.
6. Serve and enjoy.

Nutritional Value (Amount per Serving):

- Calories 154
- Fat 9.9 g
- Carbohydrates 4.6 g
- Sugar 2.4 g
- Protein 12.4 g
- Cholesterol 179 mg

Banana Oat Muffins

Preparation Time: 10 minutes
Cooking Time: 25 minutes
Serve: 6

Ingredients:
- 1 egg
- 2 tbsp butter, melted
- 1/2 tsp cinnamon
- 1 tsp vanilla
- 2 tbsp yogurt
- 1 1/2 cup oats
- 1 tsp baking powder
- 2 ripe bananas, mashed

Directions:
1. Fit the Oster oven with the rack in position 1.
2. Line the muffin tray with cupcake liners and set aside.
3. In a bowl, whisk the egg with banana, yogurt, vanilla, cinnamon, baking powder, and butter.
4. Add oats and mix well.
5. Pour mixture into the prepared muffin tray.
6. Set to bake at 350 F for 30 minutes. After 5 minutes place the muffin tray in the preheated oven.
7. Serve and enjoy.

Nutritional Value (Amount per Serving):
- Calories 164
- Fat 6.1 g
- Carbohydrates 23.9 g
- Sugar 5.5 g
- Protein 4.4 g
- Cholesterol 38 mg

Nutritious Egg Breakfast Muffins

Preparation Time: 10 minutes
Cooking Time: 20 minutes
Serve: 12

Ingredients:

- 12 eggs
- 1/2 cup baby spinach, shredded
- 1 cup cheddar cheese, shredded
- 1/4 cup mushrooms, diced & sautéed
- 1/4 red bell pepper, diced
- 1/4 tsp garlic powder
- 1 cup ham, cooked and diced
- 3 tbsp onion, diced
- 1/2 tsp seasoned salt

Directions:

1. Fit the Oster oven with the rack in position 1.
2. Spray a 12-cup muffin tray with cooking spray and set aside.
3. In a large bowl, whisk eggs with garlic powder and salt.
4. Add remaining ingredients and stir well.
5. Pour egg mixture into the prepared muffin tray.
6. Set to bake at 350 F for 25 minutes. After 5 minutes place the muffin tray in the preheated oven.
7. Serve and enjoy.

Nutritional Value (Amount per Serving):

- Calories 122
- Fat 8.5 g
- Carbohydrates 1.5 g
- Sugar 0.7 g
- Protein 9.9 g
- Cholesterol 180 mg

Choco Chip Banana Bread

Preparation Time: 10 minutes
Cooking Time: 50 minutes
Serve: 10

Ingredients:

- 2 eggs
- 3 ripe bananas
- 1 tsp vanilla
- 1 cup granulated sugar
- 1/2 cup sour cream
- 1/2 cup butter, melted
- 1/2 cup chocolate chips
- 1 1/2 cups all-purpose flour
- 1 tsp baking soda
- 1 tsp salt

Directions:

1. Fit the Oster oven with the rack in position 1.
2. In a large bowl, add bananas and mash using a fork until smooth.
3. Stir in sour cream and melted butter.
4. Add eggs, vanilla, sugar, and salt and stir well.
5. Add flour, baking soda, and salt and stir until just combined.
6. Add chocolate chips and stir well.
7. Pour batter into the greased 9*8-inch loaf pan.
8. Set to bake at 350 F for 55 minutes, after 5 minutes, place the loaf pan in the oven.
9. Slice and serve.

Nutritional Value (Amount per Serving):

- Calories 339
- Fat 15.3 g
- Carbohydrates 48 g
- Sugar 28.9 g
- Protein 4.5 g
- Cholesterol 64 mg

Easy Cheese Egg Casserole

Preparation Time: 10 minutes

Cooking Time: 40 minutes

Serve: 10

Ingredients:

- 12 eggs
- 8 oz cheddar cheese, shredded
- 1/3 cup milk
- 1/4 tsp pepper
- 1 tsp salt

Directions:

1. Fit the Oster oven with the rack in position 1.
2. Spray 9*13-inch casserole dish with cooking spray and set aside.
3. In a bowl, whisk eggs with milk, pepper, and salt.
4. Add shredded cheese and stir well.
5. Pour egg mixture into the prepared casserole dish.
6. Set to bake at 350 F for 45 minutes. After 5 minutes place the casserole dish in the preheated oven.
7. Serve and enjoy.

Nutritional Value (Amount per Serving):

- Calories 171
- Fat 12.9 g
- Carbohydrates 1.1 g
- Sugar 0.9 g
- Protein 12.6 g
- Cholesterol 221 mg

Spinach Egg Bites

Preparation Time: 10 minutes
Cooking Time: 20 minutes
Serve: 12

Ingredients:
- 8 eggs
- 1/4 cup almond milk
- 1/4 cup green onion, chopped
- 1 cup spinach, chopped
- 1 cup roasted red peppers, chopped
- 1/2 tsp salt

Directions:
1. Fit the Oster oven with the rack in position 1.
2. Spray 12-cups muffin tin with cooking spray and set aside.
3. In a bowl, whisk eggs with milk and salt.
4. Add spinach, green onion, and red peppers to the egg mixture and stir to combine.
5. Pour egg mixture into the greased muffin tin.
6. Set to bake at 350 F for 25 minutes, after 5 minutes, place muffin tin in the oven.
7. Serve and enjoy.

Nutritional Value (Amount per Serving):
- Calories 59
- Fat 4.2 g
- Carbohydrates 1.7 g
- Sugar 1.1 g
- Protein 4.1 g
- Cholesterol 109 mg

Baked Breakfast Quiche

Preparation Time: 10 minutes
Cooking Time: 45 minutes
Serve: 6

Ingredients:

- 6 eggs
- 1 cup milk
- 1 cup cheddar cheese, grated
- 1 cup tomatoes, chopped
- Pepper
- Salt

Directions:

1. Fit the Oster oven with the rack in position 1.
2. In a bowl, whisk eggs with cheese, milk, pepper, and salt. Stir in tomatoes.
3. Pour egg mixture into the greased pie dish.
4. Set to bake at 350 F for 50 minutes, after 5 minutes, place the pie dish in the oven.
5. Serve and enjoy.

Nutritional Value (Amount per Serving):

- Calories 165
- Fat 11.5 g
- Carbohydrates 3.8 g
- Sugar 3.1 g
- Protein 11.8 g
- Cholesterol 187 mg

Easy Breakfast Bake

Preparation Time: 10 minutes

Cooking Time: 45 minutes

Serve: 6

Ingredients:

- 10 eggs
- 10 bacon sliced, cooked, and crumbled
- 2 tomatoes, sliced
- 1 tbsp butter
- 3 cups baby spinach, chopped
- 1/2 tsp salt

Directions:

1. Fit the Oster oven with the rack in position 1.
2. Melt butter in a pan.
3. Add spinach and cook until spinach wilted.
4. Whisk eggs and salt in a bowl. Add spinach and whisk well.
5. Pour egg mixture into the greased 9-inch baking dish. Top with bacon and tomatoes
6. Set to bake at 350 F for 50 minutes, after 5 minutes, place the baking dish in the oven.
7. Serve and enjoy.

Nutritional Value (Amount per Serving):

- Calories 266
- Fat 21 g
- Carbohydrates 2.7 g
- Sugar 1.7 g
- Protein 18.4 g
- Cholesterol 303 mg

Breakfast Sweet Potato Hash

Preparation Time: 10 minutes

Cooking Time: 65 minutes

Serve: 6

Ingredients:

- 6 cups sweet potatoes, peeled and diced
- 1 tsp thyme
- 1 tsp onion powder
- 1 onion, diced
- 8 garlic cloves, minced
- 1/3 cup olive oil
- 1/2 tsp paprika
- 1 tbsp garlic powder
- 1/2 tsp pepper
- 2 tsp salt

Directions:

1. Fit the Oster oven with the rack in position 1.
2. Add sweet potatoes to a casserole dish and sprinkle with paprika, thyme, onion powder, garlic powder, pepper, and salt.
3. Drizzle oil over sweet potatoes and toss well.
4. Set to bake at 450 F for 60 minutes, after 5 minutes, place the casserole dish in the oven.
5. Heat 1 tbsp of olive oil in a pan over medium heat.
6. Add onion and garlic and sauté for 10 minutes.
7. Add onion and garlic mixture to the sweet potatoes and mix well.
8. Serve and enjoy.

Nutritional Value (Amount per Serving):

- Calories 294
- Fat 11.6 g
- Carbohydrates 46.5 g
- Sugar 2.1 g
- Protein 3.1 g
- Cholesterol 0 mg

Ham Egg Muffins

Preparation Time: 10 minutes

Cooking Time: 20 minutes

Serve: 12

Ingredients:

- 12 eggs
- 2 cups ham, diced
- 1 3/4 cup cheddar cheese, shredded
- 1/2 pepper
- 1/2 tsp salt

Directions:

1. Fit the Oster oven with the rack in position 1.
2. Spray 12-cups muffin tin with cooking spray and set aside.
3. In a bowl, whisk eggs with pepper and salt.
4. Stir in cheddar cheese and ham.
5. Pour egg mixture into prepared muffin tin.
6. Set to bake at 375 F for 25 minutes, after 5 minutes, place the muffin tin in the oven.
7. Serve and enjoy.

Nutritional Value (Amount per Serving):

- Calories 166
- Fat 11.8 g
- Carbohydrates 1.5 g
- Sugar 0.4 g
- Protein 13.4 g
- Cholesterol 194 mg

Lemon Blueberry Bread

Preparation Time: 10 minutes
Cooking Time: 55 minutes
Serve: 12

Ingredients:

- 2 eggs
- 1/4 cup yogurt
- 1/2 cup maple syrup
- 1 tsp baking powder
- 1 3/4 cups all-purpose flour
- 3 tbsp lemon zest, grated
- 3/4 cup blueberries
- 1/4 cup fresh lemon juice
- 1/4 cup coconut oil, melted
- 1/2 tsp salt

Directions:

1. Fit the Oster oven with the rack in position 1.
2. In a bowl, mix all-purpose flour, salt, and baking powder.
3. In a separate bowl, beat eggs with lemon juice, coconut oil, maple syrup, and yogurt.
4. Add flour mixture into the egg mixture and mix until well combined.
5. Add blueberries and lemon zest and stir well.
6. Pour batter into the greased 8*4-inch loaf pan.
7. Set to bake at 350 F for 60 minutes, after 5 minutes, place the loaf pan in the oven.
8. Slice and serve.

Nutritional Value (Amount per Serving):

- Calories 162
- Fat 5.6 g
- Carbohydrates 25.1 g
- Sugar 9.4 g
- Protein 3.2 g
- Cholesterol 28 mg

Flavorful Pumpkin Bread

Preparation Time: 10 minutes

Cooking Time: 55 minutes

Serve: 12

Ingredients:

- 2 eggs
- 8 oz pumpkin puree
- 1 3/4 cups flour
- 1 1/2 cups sugar
- 1/3 cup water
- 1/2 cup vegetable oil
- 1/8 tsp ground ginger
- 1/4 tsp ground cloves
- 1/2 tsp ground nutmeg
- 1/2 tsp ground cinnamon
- 1 tsp baking soda
- 3/4 tsp salt

Directions:

1. Fit the Oster oven with the rack in position 1.
2. In a bowl, whisk eggs, sugar, water, oil, and pumpkin puree until combined.
3. In a separate bowl, mix dry ingredients.
4. Add dry ingredient mixture into the egg mixture and mix until well combined.
5. Pour batter into the greased loaf pan.
6. Set to bake at 350 F for 60 minutes, after 5 minutes, place the loaf pan in the oven.
7. Slice and serve.

Nutritional Value (Amount per Serving):

- Calories 258
- Fat 10.1 g
- Carbohydrates 40.7 g
- Sugar 25.8 g
- Protein 3 g
- Cholesterol 27 mg

Breakfast Oatmeal Cake

Preparation Time: 10 minutes

Cooking Time: 25 minutes

Serve: 8

Ingredients:

- 2 eggs
- 1 tbsp coconut oil
- 3 tbsp yogurt
- 1/2 tsp baking powder
- 1 tsp cinnamon
- 1 tsp vanilla
- 3 tbsp honey
- 1/2 tsp baking soda
- 1 apple, peel & chopped
- 1 cup oats

Directions:

1. Fit the Oster oven with the rack in position 1.
2. Line baking dish with parchment paper and set aside.
3. Add 3/4 cup oats and remaining ingredients into the blender and blend until smooth.
4. Add remaining oats and stir well.
5. Pour mixture into the prepared baking dish.
6. Set to bake at 350 F for 30 minutes. After 5 minutes place the baking dish in the preheated oven.
7. Slice and serve.

Nutritional Value (Amount per Serving):

- Calories 114
- Fat 3.6 g
- Carbohydrates 18.2 g
- Sugar 10 g
- Protein 3.2 g
- Cholesterol 41 mg

Spinach Zucchini Egg Muffins

Preparation Time: 10 minutes
Cooking Time: 20 minutes
Serve: 12

Ingredients:

- 8 eggs
- 1 cup baby spinach, chopped
- 1 red bell pepper, diced
- 1/4 cup green onion, chopped
- 12 bacon slices, cooked and crumbled
- 2 small zucchini, sliced
- 1/4 cup almond milk
- 2 tbsp parsley, chopped
- 1 tbsp olive oil
- Pepper
- Salt

Directions:

1. Fit the Oster oven with the rack in position 1.
2. Spray 12-cups muffin tin with cooking spray and set aside.
3. Heat olive oil in a pan over medium heat.
4. Add parsley, spinach, green onion, red bell pepper to the pan and sauté until spinach is wilted.
5. In a bowl, whisk eggs with almond milk, pepper, and salt.
6. Add sautéed vegetables, bacon, and zucchini to the egg mixture and stir well.
7. Pour egg mixture into the greased muffin tin.
8. Set to bake at 350 F for 25 minutes, after 5 minutes, place muffin tin in the oven.
9. Serve and enjoy.

Nutritional Value (Amount per Serving):

- Calories 174
- Fat 13.3 g
- Carbohydrates 2.5 g
- Sugar 1.3 g
- Protein 11.3 g
- Cholesterol 130 mg

Easy Egg Quiche

Preparation Time: 10 minutes

Cooking Time: 45 minutes

Serve: 6

Ingredients:

- 8 eggs
- 4 tbsp butter, melted
- 6 oz cream cheese
- 6 oz cheddar cheese, shredded

Directions:

1. Fit the Oster oven with the rack in position 1.
2. Add eggs, cheese, butter, and cream cheese into the bowl and whisk until well combined.
3. Pour egg mixture into the greased pie dish.
4. Set to bake at 325 F for 50 minutes, after 5 minutes, place the pie dish in the oven.
5. Serve and enjoy.

Nutritional Value (Amount per Serving):

- Calories 365
- Fat 32.8 g
- Carbohydrates 1.6 g
- Sugar 0.7 g
- Protein 16.7 g
- Cholesterol 300 mg

Chapter 2: Poultry

Bacon Broccoli Chicken

Preparation Time: 10 minutes
Cooking Time: 30 minutes
Serve: 4

Ingredients:

- 4 chicken breasts, sliced in half
- 1/3 cup mozzarella cheese, shredded
- 1 cup cheddar cheese, shredded
- 1/2 cup ranch dressing
- 6 bacon slices, cooked & chopped
- 2 cups broccoli florets, chopped

Directions:

1. Fit the Oster oven with the rack in position 1.
2. Place chicken into the greased casserole dish.
3. Add ranch dressing, bacon, and broccoli on top of chicken.
4. Sprinkle cheddar cheese and mozzarella cheese on top of chicken.
5. Set to bake at 375 F for 35 minutes. After 5 minutes place the casserole dish in the preheated oven.
6. Serve and enjoy.

Nutritional Value (Amount per Serving):

- Calories 577
- Fat 32.8 g
- Carbohydrates 5.5 g
- Sugar 1.7 g
- Protein 62.2 g
- Cholesterol 192 mg

Simple & Healthy Baked Chicken Breasts

Preparation Time: 10 minutes

Cooking Time: 20 minutes

Serve: 6

Ingredients:

- 6 chicken breasts, skinless & boneless
- 1/4 tsp paprika
- 1 tsp Italian seasoning
- 2 tbsp olive oil
- 1/4 tsp pepper
- 1/2 tsp seasoning salt

Directions:

1. Fit the Oster oven with the rack in position 1.
2. Brush chicken with oil and season with paprika, Italian seasoning, pepper, and salt.
3. Place chicken breasts into the baking dish.
4. Set to bake at 400 F for 25 minutes. After 5 minutes place the baking dish in the preheated oven.
5. Serve and enjoy.

Nutritional Value (Amount per Serving):

- Calories 320
- Fat 15.7 g
- Carbohydrates 0.2 g
- Sugar 0.1 g
- Protein 42.3 g
- Cholesterol 130 mg

Pesto Chicken

Preparation Time: 10 minutes

Cooking Time: 30 minutes

Serve: 4

Ingredients:

- 4 chicken breasts, boneless & skinless
- 2 tbsp fresh basil
- 8 oz mozzarella cheese, sliced
- 2 tomatoes, sliced
- 1/2 cup pesto
- 1 tbsp garlic, minced

Directions:

1. Fit the Oster oven with the rack in position 1.
2. Place chicken into the baking dish and sprinkle with basil and garlic.
3. Pour pesto over chicken. Arrange sliced tomatoes and cheese on top of chicken.
4. Set to bake at 400 F for 35 minutes. After 5 minutes place the baking dish in the preheated oven.
5. Serve and enjoy.

Nutritional Value (Amount per Serving):

- Calories 587
- Fat 34 g
- Carbohydrates 7.1 g
- Sugar 3.6 g
- Protein 62 g
- Cholesterol 167 mg

Baked Italian Lemon Chicken

Preparation Time: 10 minutes

Cooking Time: 25 minutes

Serve: 4

Ingredients:

- 1 1/4 lbs chicken breasts, skinless and boneless
- 3 tbsp butter, melted
- 1 tsp Italian seasoning
- 1 tbsp olive oil
- 1 tbsp fresh parsley, chopped
- 2 tbsp fresh lemon juice
- 1/4 cup water
- Pepper
- Salt

Directions:

1. Fit the Oster oven with the rack in position 1.
2. Season chicken with Italian seasoning, pepper, and salt.
3. Heat oil in a pan over medium-high heat.
4. Add chicken to the pan and cook for 3-5 minutes on each side.
5. Transfer chicken to a baking dish.
6. In a small bowl, mix together butter, lemon juice, and water.
7. Pour butter mixture over chicken.
8. Set to bake at 400 F for 30 minutes. After 5 minutes place the baking dish in the preheated oven.
9. Garnish with parsley and serve.

Nutritional Value (Amount per Serving):

- Calories 382
- Fat 23.1 g
- Carbohydrates 0.4 g
- Sugar 0.3 g
- Protein 41.2 g
- Cholesterol 150 mg

Baked Spinach Cheese Chicken

Preparation Time: 10 minutes
Cooking Time: 20 minutes
Serve: 2

Ingredients:

- 2 chicken breasts, boneless & skinless
- 1/2 tsp garlic powder
- 1/4 cup sun-dried tomatoes, chopped
- 1/4 cup cheddar cheese, shredded
- 3 oz cream cheese
- 2 cups fresh spinach, chopped
- 3/4 tsp pepper
- 3/4 tsp salt

Directions:

1. Fit the Oster oven with the rack in position 1.
2. Slice the chicken breasts into the half and place them into the baking dish. Season with pepper and salt.
3. Cook spinach in the pan until wilted.
4. In a bowl, mix spinach, garlic powder, tomatoes, cheddar cheese, and cream cheese.
5. Spread spinach mixture on top of chicken breasts.
6. Set to bake at 425 F for 25 minutes. After 5 minutes place the baking dish in the preheated oven.
7. Serve and enjoy.

Nutritional Value (Amount per Serving):

- Calories 498
- Fat 30.5 g
- Carbohydrates 4.3 g
- Sugar 1.1 g
- Protein 50.2 g
- Cholesterol 192 mg

Greek Chicken Breast

Preparation Time: 10 minutes
Cooking Time: 25 minutes
Serve: 4

Ingredients:

- 4 chicken breasts, skinless & boneless
- 1 tbsp olive oil

For rub:

- 1 tsp oregano
- 1 tsp thyme
- 1 tsp parsley
- 1 tsp onion powder
- 1 tsp basil
- Pepper
- Salt

Directions:

1. Fit the Oster oven with the rack in position 2.
2. Brush chicken with olive oil.
3. In a small bowl, mix together all rub ingredients and rub all over the chicken breasts.
4. Place chicken into the air fryer basket then places the air fryer basket in the baking pan.
5. Place a baking pan on the oven rack. Set to air fry at 390 F for 25 minutes.
6. Serve and enjoy.

Nutritional Value (Amount per Serving):

- Calories 312
- Fat 14.4 g
- Carbohydrates 0.9 g
- Sugar 0.2 g
- Protein 42.4 g
- Cholesterol 130 mg

Zucchini Chicken Meatballs

Preparation Time: 10 minutes
Cooking Time: 18 minutes
Serve: 6

Ingredients:

- 1 lb ground chicken
- 1 tbsp basil, chopped
- 1/3 cup coconut flour
- 2 cups zucchini, grated
- 1 tsp dried oregano
- 1 tbsp garlic, minced
- 1 tbsp nutritional yeast
- 1 tsp cumin
- 1 tbsp dried onion flakes
- 2 eggs, lightly beaten
- Pepper
- Salt

Directions:

1. Fit the Oster oven with the rack in position 1.
2. Add all ingredients into the mixing bowl and mix until well combined.
3. Make small balls from the meat mixture and place them into the baking pan.
4. Set to bake at 400 F for 23 minutes. After 5 minutes place the baking pan in the preheated oven.
5. Serve and enjoy.

Nutritional Value (Amount per Serving):

- Calories 215
- Fat 8.5 g
- Carbohydrates 7.6 g
- Sugar 1.5 g
- Protein 26.5 g
- Cholesterol 122 mg

Meatballs

Preparation Time: 10 minutes
Cooking Time: 25 minutes
Serve: 6

Ingredients:

- 1 lb ground turkey
- 1 egg, lightly beaten
- 2 tbsp basil, chopped
- 2 tbsp coconut flour
- 1 tsp olive oil
- 1/2 tsp ground ginger
- 1/2 tsp salt

Directions:

1. Fit the Oster oven with the rack in position 1.
2. In a bowl, mix turkey, basil, coconut flour, olive oil, ginger, egg, and salt until well combined.
3. Make small balls from the meat mixture and place it into the parchment-lined baking pan.
4. Set to bake at 375 F for 30 minutes. After 5 minutes place the baking pan in the preheated oven.
5. Serve and enjoy.

Nutritional Value (Amount per Serving):

- Calories 185
- Fat 10.5 g
- Carbohydrates 2.9 g
- Sugar 0.4 g
- Protein 22.3 g
- Cholesterol 104 mg

Meatballs

Preparation Time: 10 minutes
Cooking Time: 20 minutes
Serve: 6

Ingredients:

- 2 lbs ground chicken
- 1/2 cup parmesan cheese, grated
- 1 cup breadcrumbs
- 1 egg, lightly beaten
- 1 tbsp fresh parsley, chopped
- 1 tsp Italian seasoning
- 1 tsp garlic, minced
- 2 tbsp olive oil
- Pepper
- Salt

Directions:

1. Fit the Oster oven with the rack in position 1.
2. Add all ingredients into the bowl and mix until well combined.
3. Make small balls from meat mixture and place in baking pan.
4. Set to bake at 400 F for 25 minutes. After 5 minutes place the baking pan in the preheated oven.
5. Serve and enjoy.

Nutritional Value (Amount per Serving):

- Calories 436
- Fat 19.4 g
- Carbohydrates 13.6 g
- Sugar 1.3 g
- Protein 49.5 g
- Cholesterol 168 mg

Air Fry Chicken Drumsticks

Preparation Time: 10 minutes

Cooking Time: 25 minutes

Serve: 6

Ingredients:

- 6 chicken drumsticks
- 1/2 tsp garlic powder
- 2 tbsp olive oil
- 1/2 tsp ground cumin
- 3/4 tsp paprika
- Pepper
- Salt

Directions:

1. Fit the Oster oven with the rack in position 2.
2. Add chicken drumsticks and olive oil in a large bowl and toss well.
3. Sprinkle garlic powder, paprika, cumin, pepper, and salt over chicken drumsticks and toss until well coated.
4. Place chicken drumsticks in the air fryer basket then place an air fryer basket in the baking pan.
5. Place a baking pan on the oven rack. Set to air fry at 400 F for 25 minutes.
6. Serve and enjoy.

Nutritional Value (Amount per Serving):

- Calories 120
- Fat 7.4 g
- Carbohydrates 0.4 g
- Sugar 0.1 g
- Protein 12.8 g
- Cholesterol 40 mg

Meatballs

Preparation Time: 10 minutes
Cooking Time: 20 minutes
Serve: 4

Ingredients:
- 1 lb ground turkey
- 1/4 cup basil, chopped
- 3 tbsp scallions, chopped
- 1 egg, lightly beaten
- 1/2 cup almond flour
- 1/2 tsp red pepper, crushed
- 1 tbsp lemongrass, chopped
- 1 1/2 tbsp fish sauce
- 2 garlic cloves, minced

Directions:
1. Fit the Oster oven with the rack in position 2.
2. Line the air fryer basket with parchment paper.
3. Add all ingredients into a large bowl and mix until well combined.
4. Make small balls from meat mixture and place in the air fryer basket then place the air fryer basket in the baking pan.
5. Place a baking pan on the oven rack. Set to air fry at 380 F for 20 minutes.
6. Serve and enjoy.

Nutritional Value (Amount per Serving):
- Calories 269
- Fat 15.4 g
- Carbohydrates 3.4 g
- Sugar 1.3 g
- Protein 33.9 g
- Cholesterol 157 mg

Garlic Butter Wings

Preparation Time: 10 minutes
Cooking Time: 25 minutes
Serve: 4

Ingredients:

- 1 lb chicken wings
- 1 tsp garlic powder
- 1/4 tsp pepper
- 1/2 tsp Italian seasoning
- 1/2 tsp salt

For sauce:

- 1 tbsp butter, melted
- 1/8 tsp garlic powder

Directions:

1. Fit the Oster oven with the rack in position 2.
2. In a large bowl, toss chicken wings with Italian seasoning, garlic powder, pepper, and salt.
3. Arrange chicken wings in the air fryer basket then place an air fryer basket in the baking pan.
4. Place a baking pan on the oven rack. Set to air fry at 390 F for 25 minutes.
5. In a bowl, mix melted butter and garlic powder.
6. Add chicken wings and toss until well coated.
7. Serve and enjoy.

Nutritional Value (Amount per Serving):

- Calories 246
- Fat 11.5 g
- Carbohydrates 0.7 g
- Sugar 0.2 g
- Protein 33 g
- Cholesterol 109 mg

Honey Chicken Wings

Preparation Time: 10 minutes
Cooking Time: 15 minutes
Serve: 2

Ingredients:

- 2 chicken drumsticks
- 2 tsp honey
- 2 tsp olive oil
- 2 garlic cloves, minced

Directions:

1. Fit the Oster oven with the rack in position 2.
2. In a bowl, mix honey, garlic, and olive oil.
3. Add chicken drumsticks and coat well and let it sit for 20 minutes.
4. Arrange chicken drumsticks in the air fryer basket then place an air fryer basket in the baking pan.
5. Place a baking pan on the oven rack. Set to air fry at 400 F for 15 minutes.
6. Serve and enjoy.

Nutritional Value (Amount per Serving):

- Calories 143
- Fat 7.3 g
- Carbohydrates 6.8 g
- Sugar 5.8 g
- Protein 12.9 g
- Cholesterol 40 mg

Simple Jerk Chicken Wings

Preparation Time: 10 minutes
Cooking Time: 20 minutes
Serve: 2

Ingredients:
- 1 lb chicken wings
- 1 tbsp jerk seasoning
- 1 tsp olive oil
- 1 tbsp cornstarch
- Pepper
- Salt

Directions:
1. Fit the Oster oven with the rack in position 2.
2. In a large bowl, add chicken wings.
3. Add remaining ingredients on top of chicken wings and toss to coat.
4. Add chicken wings to the air fryer basket then place an air fryer basket in the baking pan.
5. Place a baking pan on the oven rack. Set to air fry at 380 F for 20 minutes.
6. Serve and enjoy.

Nutritional Value (Amount per Serving):
- Calories 466
- Fat 19.1 g
- Carbohydrates 3.7 g
- Sugar 0 g
- Protein 65.6 g
- Cholesterol 202 mg

Garlic Chicken Wings

Preparation Time: 10 minutes

Cooking Time: 25 minutes

Serve: 2

Ingredients:
- 1 lb chicken wings
- 2 tbsp butter, melted
- 1 tbsp garlic, minced

Directions:
1. Fit the Oster oven with the rack in position 2.
2. In a large bowl, mix butter and garlic. Add chicken wings and toss to coat.
3. Add marinated chicken wings to the air fryer basket then place an air fryer basket in the baking pan.
4. Place a baking pan on the oven rack. Set to air fry at 360 F for 25 minutes.
5. Serve and enjoy.

Nutritional Value (Amount per Serving):
- Calories 539
- Fat 28.4 g
- Carbohydrates 1.4 g
- Sugar 0.1 g
- Protein 66 g
- Cholesterol 232 mg

Chapter 3: Beef, Pork & Lamb

Juicy & Tender Pork Chops

Preparation Time: 10 minutes

Cooking Time: 15 minutes

Serve: 4

Ingredients:

- 4 pork chops, boneless
- 1 tsp onion powder
- 1 tsp smoked paprika
- 1/4 cup olive oil
- 1 tsp pepper
- 2 tsp salt

Directions:

1. Fit the Oster oven with the rack in position 1.
2. Brush pork chops with oil and season with onion powder, paprika, pepper, and salt.
3. Place pork chops in a baking pan.
4. Set to bake at 400 F for 20 minutes. After 5 minutes place the baking pan in the preheated oven.
5. Serve and enjoy.

Nutritional Value (Amount per Serving):

- Calories 369
- Fat 32.6 g
- Carbohydrates 1.1 g
- Sugar 0.3 g
- Protein 18.2 g
- Cholesterol 69 mg

Meatloaf

Preparation Time: 10 minutes

Cooking Time: 20 minutes

Serve: 4

Ingredients:

- 1 lb ground pork
- 1 egg, lightly beaten
- 1 tbsp thyme, chopped
- 1/4 tsp garlic powder
- 4 tbsp breadcrumbs
- 1 onion, chopped
- 1/2 tsp Italian seasoning
- Pepper
- Salt

Directions:

1. Fit the Oster oven with the rack in position 1.
2. Add all ingredients into the mixing bowl and mix until well combined.
3. Pour meat mixture into the greased loaf pan.
4. Set to bake at 375 F for 25 minutes. After 5 minutes place the loaf pan in the preheated oven.
5. Serve and enjoy.

Nutritional Value (Amount per Serving):

- Calories 220
- Fat 5.7 g
- Carbohydrates 8.2 g
- Sugar 1.8 g
- Protein 32.4 g
- Cholesterol 124 mg

Meatballs

Preparation Time: 10 minutes
Cooking Time: 20 minutes
Serve: 6

Ingredients:

- 8 oz ground beef
- 1/2 onion, diced
- 1 egg, lightly beaten
- 1/4 cup parmesan cheese, grated
- 1/2 cup breadcrumbs
- 1/4 cup parsley, chopped
- 1 tsp garlic, minced
- 8 oz ground pork
- Pepper
- Salt

Directions:

1. Fit the Oster oven with the rack in position 1.
2. Add all ingredients into the mixing bowl and mix until well combined.
3. Make small balls from the meat mixture and place them into the baking pan.
4. Set to bake at 400 F for 25 minutes. After 5 minutes place the baking pan in the preheated oven.
5. Serve and enjoy.

Nutritional Value (Amount per Serving):

- Calories 188
- Fat 5.7 g
- Carbohydrates 7.9 g
- Sugar 1 g
- Protein 24.9 g
- Cholesterol 91 mg

Meatloaf

Preparation Time: 10 minutes
Cooking Time: 60 minutes
Serve: 8

Ingredients:

- 3 eggs
- 45 Ritz crackers, crushed
- 1 1/2 lbs lean ground beef
- 1/2 cup milk
- 4 oz sharp cheddar cheese, shredded
- 1/4 cup green pepper, diced
- 1/2 cup onion, chopped
- 1/4 tsp black pepper
- 1 tsp salt

For topping:

- 1 tsp yellow mustard
- 1/2 cup brown sugar
- 1/2 cup ketchup

Directions:

1. Fit the Oster oven with the rack in position 1.
2. In a small bowl, mix together all topping ingredients and set aside.
3. In a mixing bowl, beat the eggs then add cheese, green pepper, onion, cracker crumbs, milk pepper, and salt. Stir well to combine.
4. Add ground meat and mix well.
5. Make a loaf of meat mixture and place it into the parchment-lined baking pan.
6. Set to bake at 350 F for 35 minutes. After 5 minutes place the baking pan in the preheated oven.
7. Spread topping mixture on top of the meatloaf and bake for 30 minutes more.
8. Slice and serve.

Nutritional Value (Amount per Serving):

- Calories 316
- Fat 12.7 g
- Carbohydrates 17 g
- Sugar 13.7 g
- Protein 32.7 g
- Cholesterol 154 mg

Air Fryer Herb Pork Chops

Preparation Time: 10 minutes
Cooking Time: 15 minutes
Serve: 4

Ingredients:

- 4 pork chops
- 2 tsp oregano
- 2 tsp thyme
- 2 tsp sage
- 1 tsp garlic powder
- 1 tsp paprika
- 1 tsp rosemary
- Pepper
- Salt

Directions:

1. Fit the Oster oven with the rack in position 2.
2. Line the air fryer basket with parchment paper.
3. Mix garlic powder, paprika, rosemary, oregano, thyme, sage, pepper, and salt and rub over pork chops.
4. Place pork chops in the air fryer basket then place an air fryer basket in the baking pan.
5. Place a baking pan on the oven rack. Set to air fry at 360 F for 15 minutes.
6. Serve and enjoy.

Nutritional Value (Amount per Serving):

- Calories 266
- Fat 20.2 g
- Carbohydrates 2 g
- Sugar 0.3 g
- Protein 18.4 g
- Cholesterol 69 mg

Crispy Cracker Crusted Pork Chops

Preparation Time: 10 minutes

Cooking Time: 30 minutes

Serve: 3

Ingredients:

- 3 pork chops, boneless
- 2 tbsp milk
- 1 egg, lightly beaten
- 1/2 cup crackers, crushed
- 4 tbsp parmesan cheese, grated
- Pepper
- Salt

Directions:

1. Fit the Oster oven with the rack in position 1.
2. In a shallow bowl, whisk egg and milk.
3. In a separate shallow dish, mix cheese, crackers, pepper, and salt.
4. Dip pork chops in egg then coat with cheese mixture.
5. Place coated pork chops in a baking pan.
6. Set to bake at 350 F for 35 minutes. After 5 minutes place the baking pan in the preheated oven.
7. Serve and enjoy.

Nutritional Value (Amount per Serving):

- Calories 360
- Fat 25.9 g
- Carbohydrates 7.2 g
- Sugar 0.8 g
- Protein 23.5 g
- Cholesterol 130 mg

Meatballs

Preparation Time: 10 minutes

Cooking Time: 20 minutes

Serve: 4

Ingredients:

- 1 lb ground beef
- 2 tbsp parmesan cheese, grated
- 2 tsp Italian seasoning
- 1/4 cup rolled oats
- 1 egg, lightly beaten
- 1/2 cup spinach, chopped
- 1 tsp garlic, minced
- 1/2 onion, minced
- 4 oz mushrooms, chopped
- 3/4 cup cooked quinoa

Directions:

1. Fit the Oster oven with the rack in position 1.
2. Add all ingredients into the mixing bowl and mix until well combined.
3. Make small balls from the meat mixture and place it into the parchment-lined baking pan.
4. Set to bake at 400 F for 25 minutes. After 5 minutes place the baking pan in the preheated oven.
5. Serve and enjoy.

Nutritional Value (Amount per Serving):

- Calories 395
- Fat 12 g
- Carbohydrates 27 g
- Sugar 1.4 g
- Protein 43.3 g
- Cholesterol 146 mg

Jalapeno Basil Lamb Patties

Preparation Time: 10 minutes

Cooking Time: 8 minutes

Serve: 4

Ingredients:

- 1 lb ground lamb
- 5 basil leaves, minced
- 8 mint leaves, minced
- 1/4 cup fresh parsley, chopped
- 1 tsp dried oregano
- 1 cup goat cheese, crumbled
- 1 tbsp garlic, minced
- 1 jalapeno pepper, minced
- 1/4 tsp pepper
- 1/2 tsp kosher salt

Directions:

1. Fit the Oster oven with the rack in position 1.
2. Add all ingredients into the mixing bowl and mix until well combined.
3. Make the equal shape of patties from the meat mixture and place it into the baking pan.
4. Set to bake at 450 F for 13 minutes. After 5 minutes place the baking pan in the preheated oven.
5. Serve and enjoy.

Nutritional Value (Amount per Serving):

- Calories 296
- Fat 13.9 g
- Carbohydrates 3.7 g
- Sugar 0.5 g
- Protein 37.5 g
- Cholesterol 118 mg

Simple Burger Patties

Preparation Time: 10 minutes
Cooking Time: 8 minutes
Serve: 4

Ingredients:

- 1 lb ground beef
- 1/2 tsp garlic powder
- 1/4 tsp onion powder
- 1 tbsp soy sauce
- Pepper
- Salt

Directions:

1. Fit the Oster oven with the rack in position 2.
2. Line the air fryer basket with parchment paper.
3. Add all ingredients into the mixing bowl and mix until well combined.
4. Make four equal shape patties from the meat mixture and place in the air fryer basket then place an air fryer basket in the baking pan.
5. Place a baking pan on the oven rack. Set to air fry at 375 F for 8 minutes.
6. Serve and enjoy.

Nutritional Value (Amount per Serving):

- Calories 215
- Fat 7.1 g
- Carbohydrates 0.7 g
- Sugar 0.2 g
- Protein 34.7 g
- Cholesterol 101 mg

Meatballs

Preparation Time: 10 minutes
Cooking Time: 20 minutes
Serve: 6

Ingredients:

- 2 lbs ground beef
- 1 egg, lightly beaten
- 1 tsp cinnamon
- 2 tsp cumin
- 2 tsp coriander
- 1 tsp garlic, minced
- 1 tbsp fresh basil, chopped
- 1/4 cup fresh parsley, minced
- 1 tsp smoked paprika
- 1 tsp oregano
- 1 onion, grated
- 1/4 tsp pepper
- 1/2 tsp salt

Directions:

1. Fit the Oster oven with the rack in position 1.
2. Add all ingredients into the large mixing bowl and mix until well combined.
3. Make small balls from the meat mixture and place it into the parchment-lined baking pan.
4. Set to bake at 400 F for 25 minutes. After 5 minutes place the baking pan in the preheated oven.
5. Serve and enjoy.

Nutritional Value (Amount per Serving):

- Calories 306
- Fat 10.4 g
- Carbohydrates 3.1 g
- Sugar 0.9 g
- Protein 47.3 g
- Cholesterol 162 mg

Meatballs

Preparation Time: 10 minutes
Cooking Time: 10 minutes
Serve: 4

Ingredients:

- 2 eggs
- 1 tsp sesame oil
- 1 tsp ginger, minced
- 1 tsp garlic, minced
- 1/2 cup breadcrumbs
- 2 lbs ground pork
- 1/3 tsp red chili pepper flakes
- 1 tbsp scallions, diced
- 1 tsp soy sauce
- Pepper
- Salt

Directions:

1. Fit the Oster oven with the rack in position 2.
2. Add all ingredients into the large bowl and mix until well combined.
3. Make small balls from meat mixture and place in the air fryer basket then place the air fryer basket in the baking pan.
4. Place a baking pan on the oven rack. Set to air fry at 400 F for 10 minutes.
5. Serve and enjoy.

Nutritional Value (Amount per Serving):

- Calories 423
- Fat 12 g
- Carbohydrates 10.7 g
- Sugar 1.1 g
- Protein 64.1 g
- Cholesterol 247 mg

Flavorful Sirloin Steak

Preparation Time: 10 minutes
Cooking Time: 14 minutes
Serve: 2

Ingredients:

- 1 lb sirloin steaks
- 1/2 tsp garlic powder
- 1/2 tsp onion powder
- 1/4 tsp smoked paprika
- 1 tsp olive oil
- Pepper
- Salt

Directions:

1. Fit the Oster oven with the rack in position 2.
2. Line the air fryer basket with parchment paper.
3. Brush steak with olive oil and rub with garlic powder, onion powder, paprika, pepper, and salt.
4. Place the steak in the air fryer basket then places an air fryer basket in the baking pan.
5. Place a baking pan on the oven rack. Set to air fry at 400 F for 14 minutes.
6. Serve and enjoy.

Nutritional Value (Amount per Serving):

- Calories 447
- Fat 16.5 g
- Carbohydrates 1.2 g
- Sugar 0.4 g
- Protein 69 g
- Cholesterol 203 mg

Crispy Crusted Pork Chops

Preparation Time: 10 minutes

Cooking Time: 15 minutes

Serve: 2

Ingredients:

- 2 pork chops, bone-in
- 1 cup pork rinds, crushed
- 1/2 tsp parsley
- 1 tbsp olive oil
- 1/2 tsp garlic powder
- 1/2 tsp onion powder
- 1/2 tsp paprika

Directions:

1. Fit the Oster oven with the rack in position 2.
2. In a large bowl, mix pork rinds, garlic powder, onion powder, parsley, and paprika.
3. Brush pork chops with oil and coat with pork rind mixture.
4. place coated pork chops in air fryer basket then place air fryer basket in baking pan.
5. Place a baking pan on the oven rack. Set to air fry at 400 F for 15 minutes.
6. Serve and enjoy.

Nutritional Value (Amount per Serving):

- Calories 413
- Fat 32.7 g
- Carbohydrates 1.3 g
- Sugar 0.4 g
- Protein 28.5 g
- Cholesterol 92 mg

Meatballs

Preparation Time: 10 minutes
Cooking Time: 20 minutes
Serve: 4

Ingredients:

- 1 lb ground beef
- 1/2 cup kale, chopped
- 2 garlic cloves, finely chopped
- 1/2 onion, finely chopped
- 4 oz mushrooms, finely chopped
- 3/4 cup cooked quinoa
- 2 tsp Italian seasoning
- 1/4 cup rolled oats
- 1 egg, lightly beaten
- Pepper
- Salt

Directions:

1. Fit the Oster oven with the rack in position 2.
2. Line the air fryer basket with parchment paper.
3. Add all ingredients into a large bowl and mix until well combined.
4. Make small balls from meat mixture and place in the air fryer basket then place the air fryer basket in the baking pan.
5. Place a baking pan on the oven rack. Set to air fry at 380 F for 20 minutes.
6. Serve and enjoy.

Nutritional Value (Amount per Serving):

- Calories 388
- Fat 11.2 g
- Carbohydrates 27.9 g
- Sugar 1.4 g
- Protein 42.4 g
- Cholesterol 144 mg

Easy Pork Bites

Preparation Time: 10 minutes
Cooking Time: 15 minutes
Serve: 4

Ingredients:

- 1 lb pork belly, cut into 3/4-inch cubes
- 1/2 tsp onion powder
- 1/2 tsp garlic powder
- 1 tsp soy sauce
- Pepper
- Salt

Directions:

1. Fit the Oster oven with the rack in position 2.
2. In a mixing bowl, toss pork cubes with onion powder, garlic powder, soy sauce, pepper, and salt.
3. Place pork cubes in the air fryer basket then place an air fryer basket in the baking pan.
4. Place a baking pan on the oven rack. Set to air fry at 400 F for 15 minutes.
5. Serve and enjoy.

Nutritional Value (Amount per Serving):

- Calories 526
- Fat 30.5 g
- Carbohydrates 0.6 g
- Sugar 0.2 g
- Protein 52.5 g
- Cholesterol 131 mg

Chapter 4: Fish & Seafood

Marinated Salmon

Preparation Time: 10 minutes

Cooking Time: 10 minutes

Serve: 2

Ingredients:

- 2 salmon fillets, skinless and boneless
- For marinade:
- 2 tbsp scallions, minced
- 1 tbsp ginger, grated
- 2 garlic cloves, minced
- 2 tbsp mirin
- 2 tbsp soy sauce
- 1 tbsp olive oil

Directions:

1. Fit the Oster oven with the rack in position 2.
2. Add all marinade ingredients into the zip-lock bag and mix well.
3. Add salmon in the bag. The sealed bag shakes well and places it in the fridge for 30 minutes.
4. Arrange marinated salmon fillets in an air fryer basket then place an air fryer basket in the baking pan.
5. Place a baking pan on the oven rack. Set to air fry at 360 F for 10 minutes.
6. Serve and enjoy.

Nutritional Value (Amount per Serving):

- Calories 345
- Fat 18.2 g
- Carbohydrates 11.6 g
- Sugar 4.5 g
- Protein 36.1 g
- Cholesterol 78 mg

Paprika Cod

Preparation Time: 10 minutes
Cooking Time: 15 minutes
Serve: 4

Ingredients:

- 4 cod fillets
- 1 tsp smoked paprika
- 1/2 cup parmesan cheese, grated
- 1/2 tbsp olive oil
- 1 tsp parsley
- Pepper
- Salt

Directions:

1. Fit the Oster oven with the rack in position 1.
2. Brush fish fillets with oil and season with pepper and salt.
3. In a shallow dish, mix parmesan cheese, paprika, and parsley.
4. Coat fish fillets with cheese mixture and place into the baking dish.
5. Set to bake at 400 F for 20 minutes. After 5 minutes place the baking dish in the preheated oven.
6. Serve and enjoy.

Nutritional Value (Amount per Serving):

- Calories 125
- Fat 5 g
- Carbohydrates 0.7 g
- Sugar 0.1 g
- Protein 19.8 g
- Cholesterol 52 mg

Miso White Fish Fillets

Preparation Time: 10 minutes
Cooking Time: 10 minutes
Serve: 2

Ingredients:

- 2 cod fish fillets
- 2 tbsp brown sugar
- 2 tbsp miso
- 1 tbsp garlic, chopped

Directions:

1. Fit the Oster oven with the rack in position 2.
2. Add all ingredients to the zip-lock bag and marinate fish in the refrigerator overnight.
3. Place marinated fish fillets in the air fryer basket then place an air fryer basket in the baking pan.
4. Place a baking pan on the oven rack. Set to air fry at 350 F for 10 minutes.
5. Serve and enjoy.

Nutritional Value (Amount per Serving):

- Calories 9
- Fat 0.1 g
- Carbohydrates 0.5 g
- Sugar 0.3 g
- Protein 1.5 g
- Cholesterol 3 mg

Delicious Baked Basa

Preparation Time: 10 minutes

Cooking Time: 10 minutes

Serve: 4

Ingredients:

- 4 basa fish fillets
- 1/4 cup green onion, sliced
- 1/2 tsp garlic powder
- 1/4 tsp lemon pepper seasoning
- 4 tbsp fresh lemon juice
- 8 tsp butter, melted
- Salt

Directions:

1. Fit the Oster oven with the rack in position 1.
2. Place fish fillets into the baking dish.
3. Pour remaining ingredients over fish fillets.
4. Set to bake at 425 F for 15 minutes. After 5 minutes place the baking dish in the preheated oven.
5. Serve and enjoy.

Nutritional Value (Amount per Serving):

- Calories 214
- Fat 15.3 g
- Carbohydrates 3.8 g
- Sugar 2.3 g
- Protein 15.4 g
- Cholesterol 20 mg

Moist & Juicy Baked Cod

Preparation Time: 10 minutes

Cooking Time: 10 minutes

Serve: 2

Ingredients:

- 1 lb cod fillets
- 1 1/2 tbsp olive oil
- 3 dashes cayenne pepper
- 1 tbsp fresh lemon juice
- 1/4 tsp salt

Directions:

1. Fit the Oster oven with the rack in position 1.
2. Place fish fillets in a baking pan.
3. Drizzle with oil and lemon juice and sprinkle with cayenne pepper and salt.
4. Set to bake at 400 F for 15 minutes. After 5 minutes place the baking pan in the preheated oven.
5. Serve and enjoy.

Nutritional Value (Amount per Serving):

- Calories 275
- Fat 12.7 g
- Carbohydrates 0.4 g
- Sugar 0.2 g
- Protein 40.6 g
- Cholesterol 111 mg

Spicy Baked Shrimp

Preparation Time: 10 minutes

Cooking Time: 8 minutes

Serve: 4

Ingredients:

- 2 lbs shrimp, peeled & deveined
- 1/4 tsp cayenne pepper
- 1 tsp garlic powder
- 2 tbsp chili powder
- 2 tbsp olive oil
- 1 tsp kosher salt

Directions:

1. Fit the Oster oven with the rack in position 1.
2. Toss shrimp with remaining ingredients.
3. Transfer shrimp into the baking pan.
4. Set to bake at 400 F for 13 minutes. After 5 minutes place the baking pan in the preheated oven.
5. Serve and enjoy.

Nutritional Value (Amount per Serving):

- Calories 344
- Fat 11.5 g
- Carbohydrates 6.1 g
- Sugar 0.5 g
- Protein 52.3 g
- Cholesterol 478 mg

Italian Salmon

Preparation Time: 10 minutes
Cooking Time: 20 minutes
Serve: 4

Ingredients:

- 1 3/4 lbs salmon fillet
- 1/4 cup sun-dried tomatoes, drained
- 1 tbsp fresh dill, chopped
- 1/4 cup capers
- 1/4 cup olives, pitted and chopped
- 1/3 cup basil pesto
- 1/3 cup artichoke hearts
- 1 tsp paprika
- 1/4 tsp salt

Directions:

1. Fit the Oster oven with the rack in position 1.
2. Arrange salmon fillet in a baking pan and season with paprika and salt.
3. Pour remaining ingredients on top of salmon.
4. Set to bake at 400 F for 25 minutes. After 5 minutes place the baking pan in the preheated oven.
5. Serve and enjoy.

Nutritional Value (Amount per Serving):

- Calories 286
- Fat 13.4 g
- Carbohydrates 3.6 g
- Sugar 0.5 g
- Protein 39.6 g
- Cholesterol 88 mg

Tender & Juicy Cajun Cod

Preparation Time: 10 minutes
Cooking Time: 15 minutes
Serve: 6

Ingredients:

- 3 cod fillets, cut in half
- 1 tbsp Cajun seasoning
- 1 tbsp garlic, minced
- 1 tbsp olive oil
- 1/4 cup butter, melted
- Pepper
- Salt

Directions:

1. Fit the Oster oven with the rack in position 1.
2. Season fish fillets with pepper and salt and place in a 9*13-inch baking dish.
3. Mix together the remaining ingredients and pour over fish fillets.
4. Set to bake at 400 F for 20 minutes. After 5 minutes place the baking dish in the preheated oven.
5. Serve and enjoy.

Nutritional Value (Amount per Serving):

- Calories 126
- Fat 10.4 g
- Carbohydrates 0.5 g
- Sugar 0 g
- Protein 8.2 g
- Cholesterol 42 mg

Parmesan Salmon & Asparagus

Preparation Time: 10 minutes
Cooking Time: 20 minutes
Serve: 4

Ingredients:

- 4 salmon fillets
- 1 cup parmesan cheese, shredded
- 1 tbsp garlic, minced
- 3 tbsp olive oil
- 1 lb asparagus, ends trimmed
- 1/4 tsp pepper
- 1/4 tsp salt

Directions:

1. Fit the Oster oven with the rack in position 1.
2. Place fish fillets and asparagus in a parchment-lined baking pan.
3. Brush fish fillets with olive oil. Season with pepper and salt.
4. Sprinkle with garlic and shredded parmesan cheese on top.
5. Set to bake at 400 F for 25 minutes. After 5 minutes place the baking pan in the preheated oven.
6. Serve and enjoy.

Nutritional Value (Amount per Serving):

- Calories 424
- Fat 26.5 g
- Carbohydrates 6 g
- Sugar 2.2 g
- Protein 44.4 g
- Cholesterol 95 mg

Basil Tomato Salmon

Preparation Time: 10 minutes
Cooking Time: 20 minutes
Serve: 2

Ingredients:

- 2 salmon fillets
- 1 tomato, sliced
- 1 tbsp dried basil
- 2 tbsp parmesan cheese, grated
- 1 tbsp olive oil

Directions:

1. Fit the Oster oven with the rack in position 1.
2. Place salmon fillets in a baking dish.
3. Sprinkle basil on top of salmon fillets.
4. Arrange tomato slices on top of salmon fillets. Drizzle with oil and top with cheese.
5. Set to bake at 375 F for 25 minutes. After 5 minutes place the baking dish in the preheated oven.
6. Serve and enjoy.

Nutritional Value (Amount per Serving):

- Calories 324
- Fat 19.6 g
- Carbohydrates 1.5 g
- Sugar 0.8 g
- Protein 37.1 g
- Cholesterol 83 mg

Italian Cod

Preparation Time: 10 minutes
Cooking Time: 20 minutes
Serve: 4

Ingredients:

- 1 1/2 lbs cod fillet
- 1/4 cup olives, sliced
- 1 lb cherry tomatoes, halved
- 2 garlic cloves, crushed
- 1 small onion, chopped
- 1 tbsp olive oil
- 1/4 cup of water
- 1 tsp Italian seasoning
- Pepper
- Salt

Directions:

1. Fit the Oster oven with the rack in position 1.
2. Place fish fillets, olives, tomatoes, garlic, and onion in a baking dish. Drizzle with oil.
3. Sprinkle with Italian seasoning, pepper, and salt. Pour water into the dish.
4. Set to bake at 400 F for 25 minutes. After 5 minutes place the baking dish in the preheated oven.
5. Serve and enjoy.

Nutritional Value (Amount per Serving):

- Calories 210
- Fat 6.5 g
- Carbohydrates 7.2 g
- Sugar 3.8 g
- Protein 31.7 g
- Cholesterol 84 mg

Tasty Lemon Pepper Basa

Preparation Time: 10 minutes

Cooking Time: 12 minutes

Serve: 4

Ingredients:

- 4 basa fish fillets
- 8 tsp olive oil
- 2 tbsp fresh parsley, chopped
- 1/4 cup green onion, sliced
- 1/2 tsp garlic powder
- 1/4 tsp lemon pepper seasoning
- 4 tbsp fresh lemon juice
- Pepper
- Salt

Directions:

1. Fit the Oster oven with the rack in position 1.
2. Place fish fillets in a baking dish.
3. Pour remaining ingredients over fish fillets.
4. Set to bake at 425 F for 12 minutes. After 5 minutes place the baking dish in the preheated oven.
5. Serve and enjoy.

Nutritional Value (Amount per Serving):

- Calories 308
- Fat 21.4 g
- Carbohydrates 5.5 g
- Sugar 3.4 g
- Protein 24.1 g
- Cholesterol 0 mg

Perfect Crab Cakes

Preparation Time: 10 minutes

Cooking Time: 30 minutes

Serve: 6

Ingredients:
- 16 oz lump crab meat
- 1/4 cup celery, diced
- 1/4 cup onion, diced
- 1 cup crushed crackers
- 1 tsp old bay seasoning
- 1 tsp brown mustard
- 2/3 cup mashed avocado

Directions:
1. Fit the Oster oven with the rack in position 1.
2. Add all ingredients into the bowl and mix until just combined.
3. Make small patties from mixture and place in parchment-lined baking pan.
4. Set to bake at 350 F for 35 minutes. After 5 minutes place the baking dish in the preheated oven.
5. Serve and enjoy.

Nutritional Value (Amount per Serving):
- Calories 84
- Fat 7.7 g
- Carbohydrates 4.6 g
- Sugar 0.8 g
- Protein 11.5 g
- Cholesterol 43 mg

Spinach Scallops

Preparation Time: 10 minutes
Cooking Time: 10 minutes
Serve: 2

Ingredients:
- 8 sea scallops
- 1 tbsp fresh basil, chopped
- 1 tbsp tomato paste
- 3/4 cup heavy cream
- 12 oz frozen spinach, thawed and drained
- 1 tsp garlic, minced
- 1/2 tsp pepper
- 1/2 tsp salt

Directions:
1. Fit the Oster oven with the rack in position 1.
2. Layer spinach in the baking dish.
3. Spray scallops with cooking spray and season with pepper and salt.
4. Place scallops on top of spinach.
5. In a small bowl, mix garlic, basil, tomato paste, whipping cream, pepper, and salt and pour over scallops and spinach.
6. Set to bake at 350 F for 15 minutes. After 5 minutes place the baking dish in the preheated oven.
7. Serve and enjoy.

Nutritional Value (Amount per Serving):
- Calories 310
- Fat 18.3 g
- Carbohydrates 12.6 g
- Sugar 1.7 g
- Protein 26.5 g
- Cholesterol 101 mg

Quick Tuna Patties

Preparation Time: 10 minutes
Cooking Time: 10 minutes
Serve: 10

Ingredients:

- 15 oz can tuna, drained and flaked
- 3 tbsp parmesan cheese, grated
- 1/2 cup breadcrumbs
- 1 tbsp lemon juice
- 2 eggs, lightly beaten
- 1/2 tsp dried mixed herbs
- 1/2 tsp garlic powder
- 2 tbsp onion, minced
- 1 celery stalk, chopped
- Pepper
- Salt

Directions:

1. Fit the Oster oven with the rack in position 2.
2. Add all ingredients into the mixing bowl and mix until well combined.
3. Make patties from mixture and place in the air fryer basket then place the air fryer basket in the baking pan.
4. Place a baking pan on the oven rack. Set to air fry at 360 F for 10 minutes.
5. Serve and enjoy.

Nutritional Value (Amount per Serving):

- Calories 90
- Fat 1.8 g
- Carbohydrates 4.4 g
- Sugar 0.6 g
- Protein 13.2 g
- Cholesterol 47 mg

Chapter 5: Vegetables & Side Dishes

Cheesy Squash Casserole

Preparation Time: 10 minutes
Cooking Time: 30 minutes
Serve: 6

Ingredients:

- 2 lbs yellow summer squash, cut into chunks
- 1/2 cup liquid egg substitute
- 3/4 cup cheddar cheese, shredded
- 1/4 cup mayonnaise
- 1/4 tsp salt

Directions:

1. Fit the Oster oven with the rack in position 1.
2. Add squash in a saucepan then pour enough water in a saucepan to cover the squash. Bring to boil.
3. Turn heat to medium and cook for 10 minutes or until tender. Drain well.
4. In a large mixing bowl, combine together squash, egg substitute, mayonnaise, 1/2 cup cheese, and salt.
5. Transfer squash mixture into a greased baking dish.
6. Set to bake at 375 F for 35 minutes. After 5 minutes place the baking dish in the preheated oven.
7. Sprinkle remaining cheese on top.
8. Serve and enjoy.

Nutritional Value (Amount per Serving):

- Calories 130
- Fat 8.2 g
- Carbohydrates 7.7 g
- Sugar 3.5 g
- Protein 8 g
- Cholesterol 18 mg

Tasty Butternut Squash

Preparation Time: 10 minutes

Cooking Time: 15 minutes

Serve: 4

Ingredients:

- 4 cups butternut squash, cut into 1-inch pieces
- 1 tbsp brown sugar
- 2 tbsp olive oil
- 1 tsp Chinese 5 spice powder

Directions:

1. Fit the Oster oven with the rack in position 2.
2. Toss squash into the bowl with remaining ingredients.
3. Transfer squash in the air fryer basket then places the air fryer basket in the baking pan.
4. Place a baking pan on the oven rack. Set to air fry at 400 F for 15 minutes.
5. Serve and enjoy.

Nutritional Value (Amount per Serving):

- Calories 132
- Fat 7.1 g
- Carbohydrates 18.6 g
- Sugar 5.3 g
- Protein 1.4 g
- Cholesterol 0 mg

Baked Paprika Sweet Potatoes

Preparation Time: 10 minutes

Cooking Time: 20 minutes

Serve: 4

Ingredients:

- 3 sweet potatoes, peel and cut into 1/2-inch pieces
- 2 tbsp olive oil
- 1/2 tsp pepper
- 2 tsp smoked paprika
- 1 tsp garlic salt

Directions:

1. Fit the Oster oven with the rack in position 1.
2. Add sweet potatoes, paprika, oil, pepper, and salt into the mixing bowl and toss well.
3. Spread sweet potatoes in baking pan.
4. Set to bake at 425 F for 25 minutes. After 5 minutes place the baking pan in the preheated oven.
5. Serve and enjoy.

Nutritional Value (Amount per Serving):

- Calories 155
- Fat 7.3 g
- Carbohydrates 22.2 g
- Sugar 0.7 g
- Protein 1.5 g
- Cholesterol 0 mg

Baked Potatoes & Carrots

Preparation Time: 10 minutes

Cooking Time: 40 minutes

Serve: 2

Ingredients:

- 1/2 lb potatoes, cut into 1-inch cubes
- 1/2 onion, diced
- 1/2 tsp Italian seasoning
- 1/4 tsp garlic powder
- 1/2 lb carrots, peeled & cut into chunks
- 1 tbsp olive oil
- Pepper
- Salt

Directions:

1. Fit the Oster oven with the rack in position 1.
2. In a large bowl, toss carrots, potatoes, garlic powder, Italian seasoning, oil, onion, pepper, and salt.
3. Transfer carrot potato in baking pan.
4. Set to bake at 400 F for 45 minutes. After 5 minutes place the baking pan in the preheated oven.
5. Serve and enjoy.

Nutritional Value (Amount per Serving):

- Calories 201
- Fat 7.5 g
- Carbohydrates 32 g
- Sugar 8.2 g
- Protein 3.2 g
- Cholesterol 1 mg

Baked Vegetables

Preparation Time: 10 minutes
Cooking Time: 30 minutes
Serve: 6

Ingredients:

- 2 zucchini, sliced
- 2 tomatoes, quartered
- 6 fresh basil leaves, sliced
- 2 tsp Italian seasoning
- 2 tbsp olive oil
- 1 eggplant, sliced
- 1 onion, sliced
- 1 bell pepper, cut into strips
- Pepper
- Salt

Directions:

1. Fit the Oster oven with the rack in position 1.
2. Add all ingredients except basil leaves into the bowl and toss well.
3. Transfer vegetable mixture in parchment-lined baking pan.
4. Set to bake at 400 F for 35 minutes. After 5 minutes place the baking pan in the preheated oven.
5. Garnish with basil and serve.

Nutritional Value (Amount per Serving):

- Calories 96
- Fat 5.5 g
- Carbohydrates 11.7 g
- Sugar 6.4 g
- Protein 2.3 g
- Cholesterol 1 mg

Healthy Spinach Muffins

Preparation Time: 10 minutes

Cooking Time: 15 minutes

Serve: 12

Ingredients:

- 10 eggs
- 2 cups spinach, chopped
- 1/2 tsp dried basil
- 1 1/2 cups parmesan cheese, grated
- 1/4 tsp garlic powder
- 1/4 tsp onion powder
- Salt

Directions:

1. Fit the Oster oven with the rack in position 1.
2. Spray 12-cups muffin tin with cooking spray and set aside.
3. In a large bowl, whisk eggs with basil, garlic powder, onion powder, and salt.
4. Add cheese and spinach and stir well.
5. Pour egg mixture into the prepared muffin tin.
6. Set to bake at 400 F for 20 minutes. After 5 minutes place muffin tin in the preheated oven.
7. Serve and enjoy.

Nutritional Value (Amount per Serving):

- Calories 90
- Fat 6.1 g
- Carbohydrates 0.9 g
- Sugar 0.3 g
- Protein 8.4 g
- Cholesterol 144 mg

Tasty Hassel Back Potatoes

Preparation Time: 10 minutes

Cooking Time: 30 minutes

Serve: 4

Ingredients:

- 4 potatoes, peel & cut potato across the potato to make 1/8-inch slices
- 1/4 cup parmesan cheese, shredded
- 1 tbsp olive oil

Directions:

1. Fit the Oster oven with the rack in position 2.
2. Brush potatoes with olive oil.
3. Place potatoes in the air fryer basket then place an air fryer basket in the baking pan.
4. Place a baking pan on the oven rack. Set to air fry at 350 F for 30 minutes.
5. Sprinkle cheese on top of potatoes and serve.

Nutritional Value (Amount per Serving):

- Calories 195
- Fat 4.9 g
- Carbohydrates 33.7 g
- Sugar 2.5 g
- Protein 5.4 g
- Cholesterol 4 mg

Healthy Green Beans

Preparation Time: 10 minutes
Cooking Time: 10 minutes
Serve: 2

Ingredients:

- 8 oz green beans, trimmed and cut in half
- 1 tbsp tamari
- 1 tsp toasted sesame oil

Directions:

1. Fit the Oster oven with the rack in position 2.
2. Add all ingredients into the large bowl and toss well.
3. Transfer green beans in the air fryer basket then place an air fryer basket in the baking pan.
4. Place a baking pan on the oven rack. Set to air fry at 400 F for 10 minutes.
5. Serve and enjoy.

Nutritional Value (Amount per Serving):

- Calories 61
- Fat 2.4 g
- Carbohydrates 8.6 g
- Sugar 1.7 g
- Protein 3 g
- Cholesterol 0 mg

Brussels Sprouts & Sweet Potatoes

Preparation Time: 10 minutes

Cooking Time: 15 minutes

Serve: 6

Ingredients:

- 1 lb sweet potatoes, peeled and diced into 1/2-inch cubes
- 1 lb Brussels sprouts, remove stem & into quartered
- 2 tbsp olive oil
- 1 tsp chili powder
- Pepper
- Salt

Directions:

1. Fit the Oster oven with the rack in position 2.
2. Add Brussels sprouts, sweet potatoes, chili powder, olive oil, pepper, and salt into the mixing bowl and toss well.
3. Transfer Brussels sprouts & sweet potato mixture in air fryer basket then place air fryer basket in baking pan.
4. Place a baking pan on the oven rack. Set to air fry at 380 F for 15 minutes.
5. Serve and enjoy.

Nutritional Value (Amount per Serving):

- Calories 163
- Fat 5.1 g
- Carbohydrates 28.2 g
- Sugar 2 g
- Protein 3.8 g
- Cholesterol 0 mg

Baked Turnip & Sweet Potato

Preparation Time: 10 minutes

Cooking Time: 30 minutes

Serve: 4

Ingredients:

- 1 1/2 lbs sweet potato, sliced 1/4-inch thick
- 2 tbsp olive oil
- 1 lb turnips, sliced 1/4-inch thick
- 1 tbsp thyme, chopped
- 1 tsp paprika
- 1/4 tsp pepper
- 1/2 tsp sea salt

Directions:

1. Fit the Oster oven with the rack in position 1.
2. Add sliced sweet potatoes and turnips in a bowl and toss with seasoning and olive oil.
3. Arrange sliced sweet potatoes and turnips in baking dish.
4. Set to bake at 425 F for 35 minutes. After 5 minutes place the baking dish in the preheated oven.
5. Garnish with thyme and serve.

Nutritional Value (Amount per Serving):

- Calories 250
- Fat 7.4 g
- Carbohydrates 43.5 g
- Sugar 15.8 g
- Protein 4.5 g
- Cholesterol 0 mg

Cheese Herb Zucchini

Preparation Time: 10 minutes
Cooking Time: 15 minutes
Serve: 4

Ingredients:

- 4 zucchini, quartered
- 1/2 tsp dried oregano
- 2 tbsp fresh parsley, chopped
- 2 tbsp olive oil
- 1/2 tsp dried thyme
- 1/2 cup parmesan cheese, grated
- 1/4 tsp garlic powder
- 1/2 tsp dried basil
- Pepper
- Salt

Directions:

1. Fit the Oster oven with the rack in position 1.
2. In a small bowl, mix parmesan cheese, garlic powder, basil, oregano, thyme, pepper, and salt.
3. Arrange zucchini in baking pan and drizzle with oil and sprinkle with parmesan cheese mixture.
4. Set to bake at 350 F for 20 minutes. After 5 minutes place the baking pan in the preheated oven.
5. Garnish with parsley and serve.

Nutritional Value (Amount per Serving):

- Calories 130
- Fat 9.8 g
- Carbohydrates 7.4 g
- Sugar 3.5 g
- Protein 6.1 g
- Cholesterol 8 mg

Air Fry Garlic Baby Potatoes

Preparation Time: 10 minutes

Cooking Time: 20 minutes

Serve: 4

Ingredients:

- 1 lb baby potatoes, cut into quarters
- 1/2 tsp granulated garlic
- 1 tbsp olive oil
- 1/2 tsp dried parsley
- 1/4 tsp salt

Directions:

1. Fit the Oster oven with the rack in position 2.
2. In a mixing bowl, toss baby potatoes with oil, garlic, parsley, and salt.
3. Transfer potatoes in air fryer basket then place air fryer basket in baking pan.
4. Place a baking pan on the oven rack. Set to air fry at 350 F for 20 minutes.
5. Serve and enjoy.

Nutritional Value (Amount per Serving):

- Calories 97
- Fat 3.6 g
- Carbohydrates 14.4 g
- Sugar 0.1 g
- Protein 3 g
- Cholesterol 0 mg

Air-Fried Herb Mushrooms

Preparation Time: 10 minutes
Cooking Time: 25 minutes
Serve: 2

Ingredients:

- 1 lbs mushrooms, wash, dry, and cut into quarter
- 1 tbsp white vermouth
- 1 tsp herb de Provence
- 1/4 tsp garlic powder
- 1/2 tbsp olive oil

Directions:

1. Fit the Oster oven with the rack in position 2.
2. Add all ingredients to the bowl and toss well.
3. Transfer mushrooms in the air fryer basket then place the air fryer basket in the baking pan.
4. Place a baking pan on the oven rack. Set to air fry at 350 F for 25 minutes.
5. Serve and enjoy.

Nutritional Value (Amount per Serving):

- Calories 99
- Fat 4.5 g
- Carbohydrates 8.1 g
- Sugar 4 g
- Protein 7.9 g
- Cholesterol 0 mg

Easy Broccoli Bread

Preparation Time: 10 minutes

Cooking Time: 30 minutes

Serve: 6

Ingredients:
- 5 eggs, lightly beaten
- 3/4 cup broccoli florets, chopped
- 2 tsp baking powder
- 3 1/1 tbsp coconut flour
- 1 cup cheddar cheese, shredded

Directions:
1. Fit the Oster oven with the rack in position 1.
2. Add all ingredients into the bowl and mix well.
3. Pour egg mixture into the greased loaf pan.
4. Set to bake at 350 F for 35 minutes. After 5 minutes place the loaf pan in the preheated oven.
5. Cut the loaf into the slices and serve.

Nutritional Value (Amount per Serving):
- Calories 174
- Fat 11.3 g
- Carbohydrates 7.4 g
- Sugar 1.2 g
- Protein 11 g
- Cholesterol 156 mg

Chili Lime Sweet Potatoes

Preparation Time: 10 minutes

Cooking Time: 15 minutes

Serve: 4

Ingredients:

- 2 large sweet potatoes, peeled & cut into 1-inch pieces
- 1 tbsp chili powder
- 2 tbsp olive oil
- 2 tsp fresh lime juice
- 1 tsp cumin

Directions:

1. Fit the Oster oven with the rack in position 2.
2. In a mixing bowl, add sweet potatoes, lime juice, cumin, chili powder, and olive oil and toss well.
3. Transfer sweet potatoes in air fryer basket then place air fryer basket in baking pan.
4. Place a baking pan on the oven rack. Set to air fry at 380 F for 20 minutes.
5. Serve and enjoy.

Nutritional Value (Amount per Serving):

- Calories 132
- Fat 1.1 g
- Carbohydrates 17.1 g
- Sugar 0.8 g
- Protein 1.2 g
- Cholesterol 0 mg

Chapter 6: Snacks & Appetizers

Delicious Cauliflower Hummus

Preparation Time: 10 minutes

Cooking Time: 35 minutes

Serve: 8

Ingredients:

- 1 cauliflower head, cut into florets
- 3 tbsp olive oil
- 1/2 tsp ground cumin
- 2 tbsp fresh lemon juice
- 1/3 cup tahini
- 1 tsp garlic, chopped
- Pepper
- Salt

Directions:

1. Fit the Oster oven with the rack in position 1.
2. Spread cauliflower florets in baking pan.
3. Set to bake at 400 F for 40 minutes. After 5 minutes place the baking dish in the preheated oven.
4. Transfer roasted cauliflower into the food processor along with remaining ingredients and process until smooth.
5. Serve and enjoy.

Nutritional Value (Amount per Serving):

- Calories 115
- Fat 10.7 g
- Carbohydrates 4.2 g
- Sugar 0.9 g
- Protein 2.4 g
- Cholesterol 0 mg

Creamy Chicken Dip

Preparation Time: 10 minutes
Cooking Time: 20 minutes
Serve: 6

Ingredients:

- 2 cups chicken, cooked and shredded
- 8 oz cream cheese, softened
- 3 tbsp hot sauce
- 1/4 tsp garlic powder
- 3/4 cup sour cream
- 1/4 tsp onion powder

Directions:

1. Fit the Oster oven with the rack in position 2.
2. Add all ingredients in a large bowl and mix until well combined.
3. Transfer mixture in air fryer baking dish.
4. Set to bake at 325 F for 25 minutes. After 5 minutes place the baking dish in the preheated oven.
5. Serve and enjoy.

Nutritional Value (Amount per Serving):

- Calories 265
- Fat 20.7 g
- Carbohydrates 2.5 g
- Sugar 0.3 g
- Protein 17.4 g
- Cholesterol 90 mg

Baked Almonds

Preparation Time: 10 minutes

Cooking Time: 20 minutes

Serve: 6

Ingredients:

- 1 1/2 cups raw almonds
- 1/2 tsp cayenne
- 1/4 tsp onion powder
- 1/4 tsp dried basil
- 2 tbsp butter, melted
- 1/2 tsp garlic powder
- 1/2 tsp cumin
- 1 1/2 tsp chili powder
- 1/2 tsp sea salt

Directions:

1. Fit the Oster oven with the rack in position 1.
2. Add almonds and remaining ingredients into the mixing bowl and toss well.
3. Spread almonds in baking pan.
4. Set to bake at 350 F for 25 minutes. After 5 minutes place the baking pan in the preheated oven.
5. Serve and enjoy.

Nutritional Value (Amount per Serving):

- Calories 176
- Fat 15.9 g
- Carbohydrates 5.9 g
- Sugar 1.2 g
- Protein 5.2 g
- Cholesterol 10 mg

Bacon Cheese Jalapeno Poppers

Preparation Time: 10 minutes

Cooking Time: 5 minutes

Serve: 5

Ingredients:

- 10 fresh jalapeno peppers, cut in half and remove seeds
- 1/4 cup cheddar cheese, shredded
- 5 oz cream cheese, softened
- ¼ tsp paprika
- 2 bacon slices, cooked and crumbled

Directions:

1. Fit the Oster oven with the rack in position 2.
2. In a bowl, mix bacon, cream cheese, paprika and cheddar cheese.
3. Stuff cheese mixture into each jalapeno.
4. Place stuffed jalapeno halved in air fryer basket then place air fryer basket in baking pan.
5. Place a baking pan on the oven rack. Set to air fry at 370 F for 5 minutes.
6. Serve and enjoy.

Nutritional Value (Amount per Serving):

- Calories 176
- Fat 15.7 g
- Carbohydrates 3.2 g
- Sugar 1 g
- Protein 6.2 g
- Cholesterol 47 mg

Cheddar Dill Mushrooms

Preparation Time: 10 minutes
Cooking Time: 5 minutes
Serve: 6

Ingredients:

- 9 oz mushrooms, cut stems
- 6 oz mozzarella cheese, shredded
- 1 tbsp butter
- 1 tsp dried parsley
- 1/2 tsp salt

Directions:

1. Fit the Oster oven with the rack in position 2.
2. Add parsley, cheese, butter, and salt into the bowl and mix until well combined.
3. Stuff cheese mixture into the mushroom caps and place in the air fryer basket then place an air fryer basket in the baking pan.
4. Place a baking pan on the oven rack. Set to air fry at 400 F for 5 minutes.
5. Serve and enjoy.

Nutritional Value (Amount per Serving):

- Calories 141
- Fat 11.5 g
- Carbohydrates 1.9 g
- Sugar 0.9 g
- Protein 8.5 g
- Cholesterol 35 mg

Cheesy Spinach Dip

Preparation Time: 10 minutes
Cooking Time: 20 minutes
Serve: 12

Ingredients:

- 3 oz frozen spinach, defrosted & chopped
- 1 cup sour cream
- 1 tsp garlic salt
- 2 cups cheddar cheese, shredded
- 8 oz cream cheese

Directions:

1. Fit the Oster oven with the rack in position 1.
2. Add all ingredients into the mixing bowl and mix well.
3. Transfer mixture into the baking dish.
4. Set to bake at 350 F for 25 minutes. After 5 minutes place the baking dish in the preheated oven.
5. Serve and enjoy.

Nutritional Value (Amount per Serving):

- Calories 185
- Fat 16.9 g
- Carbohydrates 2 g
- Sugar 0.3 g
- Protein 7 g
- Cholesterol 49 mg

Garlic Cauliflower Florets

Preparation Time: 10 minutes

Cooking Time: 20 minutes

Serve: 4

Ingredients:
- 5 cups cauliflower florets
- 6 garlic cloves, chopped
- 4 tablespoons olive oil
- 1/2 tsp cumin powder
- 1/2 tsp salt

Directions:
1. Fit the Oster oven with the rack in position 2.
2. Add all ingredients into the large bowl and toss well.
3. Add cauliflower florets in air fryer basket then place air fryer basket in baking pan.
4. Place a baking pan on the oven rack. Set to air fry at 400 F for 20 minutes.
5. Serve and enjoy.

Nutritional Value (Amount per Serving):
- Calories 159
- Fat 14.2 g
- Carbohydrates 8.2 g
- Sugar 3.1 g
- Protein 2.8 g
- Cholesterol 0 mg

Kale Chips

Preparation Time: 10 minutes
Cooking Time: 5 minutes
Serve: 2

Ingredients:

- 1 bunch of kale, remove stem and cut into pieces
- 1 tsp olive oil
- 1/2 tsp salt

Directions:

1. Fit the Oster oven with the rack in position 2.
2. Add all ingredients into the large bowl and toss well.
3. Transfer kale mixture in air fryer basket then places air fryer basket in baking pan.
4. Place a baking pan on the oven rack. Set to air fry at 370 F for 5 minutes.
5. Serve and enjoy.

Nutritional Value (Amount per Serving):

- Calories 41
- Fat 2.3 g
- Carbohydrates 4.4 g
- Sugar 0 g
- Protein 1.3 g
- Cholesterol 0 mg

Shrimp Kebabs

Preparation Time: 10 minutes
Cooking Time: 8 minutes
Serve: 2

Ingredients:
- 1 cup shrimp
- 1/4 tsp pepper
- 1/8 tsp salt
- 1 lime juice
- 1 garlic clove, minced

Directions:
1. Fit the Oster oven with the rack in position 2.
2. Add shrimp and remaining ingredients into the bowl and toss well.
3. Thread shrimp onto the skewers and place in the air fryer basket then place an air fryer basket in the baking pan.
4. Place a baking pan on the oven rack. Set to air fry at 350 F for 8 minutes.
5. Serve and enjoy.

Nutritional Value (Amount per Serving):
- Calories 59
- Fat 0.8 g
- Carbohydrates 3.2 g
- Sugar 0.4 g
- Protein 9.9 g
- Cholesterol 90 mg

Spicy Chicken Wings

Preparation Time: 10 minutes
Cooking Time: 16 minutes
Serve: 6

Ingredients:

- 1/2 lb chicken wings
- 2 tsp ginger powder
- 1 tsp paprika
- 1/3 cup hot sauce
- 2 tsp garlic powder
- Pepper
- Salt

Directions:

1. Fit the Oster oven with the rack in position 2.
2. Toss chicken wings with paprika, garlic powder, pepper, ginger powder, and salt.
3. Add chicken wings to the air fryer basket then place an air fryer basket in the baking pan.
4. Place a baking pan on the oven rack. Set to air fry at 360 F for 16 minutes.
5. Serve with hot sauce.

Nutritional Value (Amount per Serving):

- Calories 104
- Fat 2.9 g
- Carbohydrates 5.8 g
- Sugar 3.9 g
- Protein 11.2 g
- Cholesterol 34 mg

Artichoke Cashews Spinach Dip

Preparation Time: 10 minutes

Cooking Time: 20 minutes

Serve: 10

Ingredients:

- 28 oz can artichokes, drained and rinsed
- 1 small onion, diced
- 4 garlic cloves
- 1 1/2 cups cashews
- 1 tsp olive oil
- 4 cups fresh spinach
- 2 tbsp fresh lemon juice
- 1/4 cup nutritional yeast
- 1 1/2 cups milk
- 1 1/2 tsp salt

Directions:

1. Fit the Oster oven with the rack in position 2.
2. Soak cashews in boiling water for 5 minutes. Drain well.
3. Heat oil in a pan over medium heat. Add onion and garlic and sauté for 2-3 minutes.
4. Remove pan from heat and set aside.
5. Add soaked cashews, milk, nutritional yeast, lemon juice, and salt into the blender and blend until smooth.
6. Add sautéed garlic onion, artichokes, and spinach and blend for few minutes until getting chunky texture.
7. Transfer blended mixture into the baking dish.
8. Set to bake at 425 F for 25 minutes. After 5 minutes place the baking dish in the preheated oven.
9. Serve and enjoy.

Nutritional Value (Amount per Serving):

- Calories 205
- Fat 11.3 g
- Carbohydrates 21.4 g
- Sugar 3.9 g
- Protein 9 g
- Cholesterol 3 mg

Air Fryer Radish Chips

Preparation Time: 10 minutes
Cooking Time: 15 minutes
Serve: 12

Ingredients:

- 1 lb radish, wash and slice into chips
- 1/4 tsp pepper
- 2 tbsp olive oil
- 1 tsp salt

Directions:

1. Fit the Oster oven with the rack in position 2.
2. Add all ingredients into the large bowl and toss well.
3. Add radish slices to the air fryer basket then place an air fryer basket in baking pan.
4. Place a baking pan on the oven rack. Set to air fry at 375 F for 15 minutes.
5. Serve and enjoy.

Nutritional Value (Amount per Serving):

- Calories 26
- Fat 2.4 g
- Carbohydrates 1.3 g
- Sugar 0.7 g
- Protein 0.3 g
- Cholesterol 0 mg

Coconut Broccoli Pop-Corn

Preparation Time: 10 minutes

Cooking Time: 6 minutes

Serve: 4

Ingredients:

- 2 cups broccoli florets
- 4 eggs yolks
- 2 cups coconut flour
- 1/4 cup butter, melted
- Pepper
- Salt

Directions:

1. Fit the Oster oven with the rack in position 2.
2. In a bowl whisk egg yolks with melted butter, pepper, and salt. Add coconut flour and stir to combine.
3. Coat each broccoli floret with egg mixture and place in the air fryer basket then place an air fryer basket in the baking pan.
4. Place a baking pan on the oven rack. Set to air fry at 400 F for 6 minutes.
5. Serve and enjoy.

Nutritional Value (Amount per Serving):

- Calories 201
- Fat 17.2 g
- Carbohydrates 7.7 g
- Sugar 1.4 g
- Protein 5.1 g
- Cholesterol 240 mg

Habanero Chicken Wings

Preparation Time: 10 minutes

Cooking Time: 16 minutes

Serve: 6

Ingredients:

- 1 1/2 lbs chicken wings
- 2 tbsp habanero hot sauce
- 2 garlic cloves, chopped
- 1 tsp pepper
- 1 tsp garlic salt
- 1 tsp cayenne pepper
- 1/2 tbsp soy sauce

Directions:

1. Fit the Oster oven with the rack in position 2.
2. Add chicken wings into the large bowl and toss with remaining ingredients.
3. Transfer chicken wings in air fryer basket then place air fryer basket in baking pan.
4. Place a baking pan on the oven rack. Set to air fry at 360 F for 16 minutes.
5. Serve and enjoy.

Nutritional Value (Amount per Serving):

- Calories 226
- Fat 8.5 g
- Carbohydrates 2.2 g
- Sugar 0.2 g
- Protein 33.1 g
- Cholesterol 101 mg

Zucchini Coconut Bites

Preparation Time: 10 minutes

Cooking Time: 10 minutes

Serve: 6

Ingredients:

- 4 zucchini, grated and squeeze out all liquid
- 1 cup shredded coconut
- 1 egg, lightly beaten
- 1 tsp Italian seasoning
- 1/2 cup parmesan cheese, grated

Directions:

1. Fit the Oster oven with the rack in position 2.
2. Add all ingredients into the bowl and mix until well combined.
3. Make small balls from the zucchini mixture and place in the air fryer basket then place the air fryer basket in the baking pan.
4. Place a baking pan on the oven rack. Set to air fry at 400 F for 10 minutes.
5. Serve and enjoy.

Nutritional Value (Amount per Serving):

- Calories 105
- Fat 7.3 g
- Carbohydrates 6.8 g
- Sugar 3.2 g
- Protein 5.4 g
- Cholesterol 33 mg

Chapter 7: Desserts

Cinnamon Apple Crisp

Preparation Time: 10 minutes
Cooking Time: 35 minutes
Serve: 4

Ingredients:

- 1/8 tsp ground clove
- 1/8 tsp ground nutmeg
- 2 tbsp honey
- 4 1/2 cups apples, diced
- 1 tsp ground cinnamon
- 1 tbsp cornstarch
- 1 tsp vanilla
- 1/2 lemon juice

For topping:

- 1 cup rolled oats
- 1/3 cup coconut oil, melted
- 1 tsp cinnamon
- 1/3 cup honey
- 1/2 cup almond flour

Directions:

1. Fit the Oster oven with the rack in position 1.
2. In a medium bowl, mix apples, vanilla, lemon juice, and honey. Sprinkle spices and cornstarch on top and stir well.
3. Pour apple mixture into the greased baking dish.
4. In a small bowl, mix together coconut oil, cinnamon, almond flour, oats, and honey and spread on top of apple mixture.
5. Set to bake at 350 F for 40 minutes. After 5 minutes place the baking dish in the preheated oven.
6. Serve and enjoy.

Nutritional Value (Amount per Serving):

- Calories 450
- Fat 21 g
- Carbohydrates 65 g
- Sugar 40 g
- Protein 4 g
- Cholesterol 0 mg

Peanut Butter Muffins

Preparation Time: 10 minutes
Cooking Time: 20 minutes
Serve: 12

Ingredients:

- 1 cup peanut butter
- 1/2 cup maple syrup
- 1/2 cup of cocoa powder
- 1 cup applesauce
- 1 tsp baking soda
- 1 tsp vanilla

Directions:

1. Fit the Oster oven with the rack in position 1.
2. Line 12-cups muffin tin with cupcake liners and set aside.
3. Add all ingredients into the blender and blend until smooth.
4. Pour blended mixture into the prepared muffin tin.
5. Set to bake at 350 F for 25 minutes. After 5 minutes place muffin tin in the preheated oven.
6. Serve and enjoy.

Nutritional Value (Amount per Serving):

- Calories 178
- Fat 11.3 g
- Carbohydrates 17.3 g
- Sugar 12 g
- Protein 6.1 g
- Cholesterol 0 mg

Apple Cake

Preparation Time: 10 minutes
Cooking Time: 45 minutes
Serve: 12

Ingredients:

- 2 cups apples, peeled and chopped
- 1/4 cup sugar
- 1/4 cup butter, melted
- 12 oz apple juice
- 3 cups all-purpose flour
- 3 tsp baking powder
- 1 1/2 tbsp ground cinnamon
- 1 tsp Salt

Directions:

1. Fit the Oster oven with the rack in position 1.
2. In a large bowl, mix together flour, salt, sugar, cinnamon, and baking powder.
3. Add melted butter and apple juice and mix until well combined.
4. Add apples and fold well.
5. Pour batter into the greased baking dish.
6. Set to bake at 350 F for 45 minutes. After 5 minutes place the baking dish in the preheated oven.
7. Serve and enjoy.

Nutritional Value (Amount per Serving):

- Calories 200
- Fat 4 g
- Carbohydrates 38 g
- Sugar 11 g
- Protein 3 g
- Cholesterol 10 mg

Vanilla Butter Cake

Preparation Time: 10 minutes
Cooking Time: 30 minutes
Serve: 8

Ingredients:

- 1 egg, beaten
- 1/2 tsp vanilla
- 3/4 cup sugar
- 1 cup all-purpose flour
- 1/2 cup butter, softened

Directions:

1. Fit the Oster oven with the rack in position 1.
2. In a mixing bowl, mix together sugar and butter.
3. Add egg, flour, and vanilla and mix until combined.
4. Pour batter into the greased baking dish.
5. Set to bake at 350 F for 35 minutes. After 5 minutes place the baking dish in the preheated oven.
6. Slice and serve.

Nutritional Value (Amount per Serving):

- Calories 211
- Fat 11 g
- Carbohydrates 27 g
- Sugar 16 g
- Protein 2 g
- Cholesterol 45 mg

Vanilla Lemon Cupcakes

Preparation Time: 10 minutes
Cooking Time: 15 minutes
Serve: 6

Ingredients:

- 1 egg
- 1/2 cup milk
- 2 tbsp canola oil
- 1/4 tsp baking soda
- 3/4 tsp baking powder
- 1 tsp lemon zest, grated
- 1/2 cup sugar
- 1 cup flour
- 1/2 tsp vanilla
- 1/2 tsp salt

Directions:

1. Fit the Oster oven with the rack in position 1.
2. Line 12-cups muffin tin with cupcake liners and set aside.
3. In a bowl, whisk egg, vanilla, milk, oil, and sugar until creamy.
4. Add remaining ingredients and stir until just combined.
5. Pour batter into the prepared muffin tin.
6. Set to bake at 350 F for 20 minutes. After 5 minutes place muffin tin in the preheated oven.
7. Serve and enjoy.

Nutritional Value (Amount per Serving):

- Calories 200
- Fat 6 g
- Carbohydrates 35 g
- Sugar 17 g
- Protein 3 g
- Cholesterol 30 mg

Easy Blueberry Muffins

Preparation Time: 10 minutes

Cooking Time: 30 minutes

Serve: 12

Ingredients:

- 5.5 oz plain yogurt
- ½ cup fresh blueberries
- 2 tsp baking powder, gluten-free
- ¼ cup Swerve
- 2 ½ cups almond flour
- ½ tsp vanilla
- 3 eggs
- Pinch of salt

Directions:

1. Fit the Oster oven with the rack in position 1.
2. Line 6-cups muffin tin with cupcake liners and set aside.
3. In a bowl, whisk egg, yogurt, vanilla, and salt until smooth.
4. Add flour, swerve and baking powder and blend again until smooth.
5. Add blueberries and stir well.
6. Pour batter into the prepared muffin tin.
7. Set to bake at 325 F for 35 minutes. After 5 minutes place muffin tin in the preheated oven.
8. Serve and enjoy.

Nutritional Value (Amount per Serving):

- Calories 63
- Fat 4.2 g
- Carbohydrates 3.6 g
- Sugar 1.8 g
- Protein 3.4 g
- Cholesterol 42 mg

Simple Lemon Pie

Preparation Time: 10 minutes

Cooking Time: 45 minutes

Serve: 8

Ingredients:

- 3 eggs
- 3.5 oz butter, melted
- 3 lemon juice
- 1 lemon zest, grated
- 4 oz erythritol
- 5.5 oz almond flour
- Salt

Directions:

1. Fit the Oster oven with the rack in position 1.
2. In a bowl, mix together butter, 1 oz sweetener, 3 oz almond flour, and salt.
3. Transfer the dough in a pie dish and spread evenly and bake for 20 minutes.
4. In a separate bowl, mix together eggs, lemon juice, lemon zest, remaining flour, sweetener, and salt.
5. Pour egg mixture on prepared crust.
6. Set to bake at 350 F for 35 minutes. After 5 minutes place the pie dish in the preheated oven.
7. Slice and serve.

Nutritional Value (Amount per Serving):

- Calories 229
- Fat 21.5 g
- Carbohydrates 5.3 g
- Sugar 1.4 g
- Protein 6.5 g
- Cholesterol 88 mg

Mini Brownie Muffins

Preparation Time: 10 minutes

Cooking Time: 15 minutes

Serve: 6

Ingredients:

- 3 eggs
- 1/2 cup Swerve
- 1 cup almond flour
- 1 tbsp gelatin
- 1/3 cup butter, melted
- 1/3 cup cocoa powder

Directions:

1. Fit the Oster oven with the rack in position 1.
2. Line 6-cups muffin tin with cupcake liners and set aside.
3. Add all ingredients into the mixing bowl and stir until well combined.
4. Pour mixture into the prepared muffin tin.
5. Set to bake at 350 F for 20 minutes. After 5 minutes place muffin tin in the preheated oven.
6. Serve and enjoy.

Nutritional Value (Amount per Serving):

- Calories 163
- Fat 15.4 g
- Carbohydrates 4 g
- Sugar 0.4 g
- Protein 5.8 g
- Cholesterol 109 mg

Coconut Butter Apple Bars

Preparation Time: 10 minutes

Cooking Time: 45 minutes

Serve: 8

Ingredients:

- 1 tbsp ground flax seed
- 1/4 cup coconut butter, softened
- 1 cup pecans
- 1 cup of water
- 1/4 cup dried apples
- 1 1/2 tsp baking powder
- 1 1/2 tsp cinnamon
- 1 tsp vanilla
- 2 tbsp swerve

Directions:

1. Fit the Oster oven with the rack in position 1.
2. Add all ingredients into the blender and blend until smooth.
3. Pour blended mixture into the greased baking dish.
4. Set to bake at 350 F for 50 minutes. After 5 minutes place the baking dish in the preheated oven.
5. Slice and serve.

Nutritional Value (Amount per Serving):

- Calories 161
- Fat 15 g
- Carbohydrates 6 g
- Sugar 2 g
- Protein 2 g
- Cholesterol 0 mg

Vanilla Banana Brownies

Preparation Time: 10 minutes
Cooking Time: 20 minutes
Serve: 12

Ingredients:
- 1 egg
- 1 cup all-purpose flour
- 4 oz white chocolate
- 1/4 cup butter
- 1 tsp vanilla extract
- 1/2 cup granulated sugar
- 2 medium bananas, mashed
- 1/4 tsp salt

Directions:
1. Fit the Oster oven with the rack in position 1.
2. Add white chocolate and butter in a microwave-safe bowl and microwave for 30 seconds. Stir until melted.
3. Stir in sugar. Add mashed bananas, eggs, vanilla, and salt and mix until combined.
4. Add flour and mix until just combined.
5. Pour batter into the greased baking dish.
6. Set to bake at 350 F for 25 minutes. After 5 minutes place the baking dish in the preheated oven.
7. Slice and serve.

Nutritional Value (Amount per Serving):
- Calories 178
- Fat 7.4 g
- Carbohydrates 26.4 g
- Sugar 16.4 g
- Protein 2.3 g
- Cholesterol 26 mg

Tasty Gingersnap Cookies

Preparation Time: 10 minutes

Cooking Time: 10 minutes

Serve: 8

Ingredients:

- 1 egg
- 1/2 tsp ground cinnamon
- 1/2 tsp ground ginger
- 1 tsp baking powder
- 3/4 cup erythritol
- 1/2 tsp vanilla
- 1/8 tsp ground cloves
- 1/4 tsp ground nutmeg
- 2/4 cup butter, melted
- 1 1/2 cups almond flour
- Pinch of salt

Directions:

1. Fit the Oster oven with the rack in position 1.
2. In a mixing bowl, mix together all dry ingredients.
3. In another bowl, mix together all wet ingredients.
4. Add dry ingredients to the wet ingredients and mix until a dough-like mixture is formed.
5. Cover and place in the refrigerator for 30 minutes.
6. Make cookies from dough and place onto a parchment-lined baking pan.
7. Set to bake at 350 F for 15 minutes. After 5 minutes place the baking pan in the preheated oven.
8. Serve and enjoy.

Nutritional Value (Amount per Serving):

- Calories 142
- Fat 14.7 g
- Carbohydrates 1.8 g
- Sugar 0.3 g
- Protein 2 g
- Cholesterol 51 mg

Delicious Raspberry Cobbler

Preparation Time: 10 minutes

Cooking Time: 10 minutes

Serve: 6

Ingredients:

- 1 egg, lightly beaten
- 1 cup raspberries, sliced
- 2 tsp swerve
- 1/2 tsp vanilla
- 1 tbsp butter, melted
- 1 cup almond flour

Directions:

1. Fit the Oster oven with the rack in position 1.
2. Add raspberries into the baking dish.
3. Sprinkle sweetener over raspberries.
4. Mix together almond flour, vanilla, and butter in the bowl.
5. Add egg in almond flour mixture and stir well to combine.
6. Spread almond flour mixture over sliced raspberries.
7. Set to bake at 350 F for 15 minutes. After 5 minutes place the baking dish in the preheated oven.
8. Serve and enjoy.

Nutritional Value (Amount per Serving):

- Calories 66
- Fat 5 g
- Carbohydrates 3 g
- Sugar 1 g
- Protein 2 g
- Cholesterol 32 mg

Almond Butter Cookies

Preparation Time: 10 minutes
Cooking Time: 15 minutes
Serve: 15

Ingredients:

- 1 egg
- 1/2 cup erythritol
- 1 cup almond butter
- 1 tsp vanilla
- Pinch of salt

Directions:

1. Fit the Oster oven with the rack in position 1.
2. Add all ingredients into the large bowl and mix until well combined.
3. Make cookies from bowl mixture and place on a parchment-lined baking pan.
4. Set to bake at 350 F for 20 minutes. After 5 minutes place the baking pan in the preheated oven.
5. Serve.

Nutritional Value (Amount per Serving):

- Calories 12
- Fat 0.9 g
- Carbohydrates 0.3 g
- Sugar 0.1 g
- Protein 0.6 g
- Cholesterol 11 mg

Strawberry Muffins

Preparation Time: 10 minutes
Cooking Time: 20 minutes
Serve: 12

Ingredients:

- 4 eggs
- 1/4 cup water
- 1/2 cup butter, melted
- 2 tsp baking powder
- 2 cups almond flour
- 2/3 cup strawberries, chopped
- 2 tsp vanilla
- 1/4 cup erythritol
- Pinch of salt

Directions:

1. Fit the Oster oven with the rack in position 1.
2. Line 12-cups muffin tin with cupcake liners and set aside.
3. In a medium bowl, mix together almond flour, baking powder, and salt.
4. In a separate bowl, whisk eggs, sweetener, vanilla, water, and butter.
5. Add almond flour mixture into the egg mixture and mix until well combined.
6. Add strawberries and stir well.
7. Pour batter into the prepared muffin tin.
8. Set to bake at 350 F for 25 minutes. After 5 minutes place muffin tin in the preheated oven.
9. Serve and enjoy.

Nutritional Value (Amount per Serving):

- Calories 201
- Fat 18.5 g
- Carbohydrates 5.2 g
- Sugar 1.3 g
- Protein 6 g
- Cholesterol 75 mg

Almond Pecan Cookies

Preparation Time: 10 minutes

Cooking Time: 20 minutes

Serve: 16

Ingredients:

- 1/2 cup butter
- 1 tsp vanilla
- 2 tsp gelatin
- 2/3 cup Swerve
- 1 cup pecans
- 1/3 cup coconut flour
- 1 cup almond flour

Directions:

1. Fit the Oster oven with the rack in position 1.
2. Add butter, vanilla, gelatin, swerve, coconut flour, and almond flour into the food processor and process until crumbs form.
3. Add pecans and process until chopped.
4. Make cookies from prepared mixture and place onto a parchment-lined baking pan.
5. Set to bake at 350 F for 25 minutes. After 5 minutes place the baking pan in the preheated oven.
6. Serve and enjoy.

Nutritional Value (Amount per Serving):

- Calories 101
- Fat 10.2 g
- Carbohydrates 1.4 g
- Sugar 0.3 g
- Protein 1.8 g
- Cholesterol 15 mg

Conclusion

In truth, the Digital Air Fryer Oven cook food by blasting with circulating hot air. The method is fast, convenient, and can be surprisingly good~if you have the right recipe. What really drew us to this appliance was the variety of what you can make in it, effortlessly and without having to enlist numerous pots and pans.

The Complete Digital Air Fryer Oven Cookbook goes beyond fried foods to give you inspired meals that are baked, grilled, roasted, and more. Get the best possible results from your Digital Air Fryer Oven and discover the best ways to use it, not just frying!

www.ingramcontent.com/pod-product-compliance
Lightning Source LLC
Chambersburg PA
CBHW081403070526
44583CB00020B/2651